Putting **Essential Understanding** of

Addition and Subtraction

into **Practice**

in

Prekindergarten–Grade 2

Janet H. Caldwell
Rowan University
Glassboro, New Jersey

Beth Kobett
Stevenson University
Stevenson, Maryland

Karen Karp
University of Louisville
Louisville, Kentucky

Karen Karp
Volume Editor
University of Louisville
Louisville, Kentucky

Barbara J. Dougherty
Series Editor
University of Missouri
Columbia, Missouri

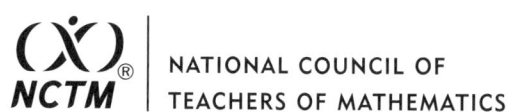

NATIONAL COUNCIL OF
TEACHERS OF MATHEMATICS

www.nctm.org/more4u
Access code: AAS14540

Library of Congress Cataloging-in-Publication Data

Caldwell, Janet H., author.
  Putting essential understanding of addition and subtraction into practice in
prekindergarten–grade 2 / by Janet H. Caldwell, Rowan University, Glassboro, New Jersey,
Beth Kobett, Stevenson University, Stevenson, Maryland, and Karen Karp, University
of Louisville, Louisville, Kentucky ; Karen Karp, volume editor, University of Louisville,
Louisville, Kentucky.
      pages cm. – (Putting essential understanding into practice series)
  Includes bibliographical references.
  ISBN 978-0-87353-730-8
1. Addition–Study and teaching (Early childhood) 2. Addition–Study and teaching (Primary)
3. Subtraction–Study and teaching (Early childhood) 4. Subtraction–Study and teaching
(Primary) I. Kobett, Beth McCord, author. II. Karp, Karen S., author. III. Title.
  QA115.C16 2014
  372.7′049–dc 3

                        2013050510

The National Council of Teachers of Mathematics is the public voice of mathematics
education, providing vision, leadership, and professional development to support teachers
in ensuring equitable mathematics learning of the highest quality for all students.

Printed in the United States of America

Contents

Chapter 3
Strategies for Basic Facts for Addition and Subtraction 67

Chapter 4
Understanding Multi-Digit Addition and Subtraction 97

Chapter 5
Looking Back and Looking Ahead with Addition and Subtraction 123

Appendix 1
The Big Ideas and Essential Understandings for Addition and Subtraction.. 133

Appendix 2
Resources for Teachers.. 135

Appendix 3
Tasks 141

References 149

Accompanying Materials at More4U

Appendix 1
The Big Ideas and Essential Understandings for Addition and Subtraction

Appendix 2
Resources for Teachers

Appendix 3
Tasks

Count, Sort, Compare

How Can You Show ____?

How Many Ways Can They Land?

Macaroni Squeeze Game

Where Are the Guinea Pigs?

Hen and Egg Game

Dot Cards

Corduroy's Pocket, Inside and Out

How Are They Alike?

How Many *Won't Get*?

Translation Task

Sort and Group Basic Facts

Spin, Circle, and Solve

Ring Facts

Livescribe Pencast for "Where Are the Guinea Pigs?" (link)

Foreword

Teaching mathematics in prekindergarten–grade 12 requires knowledge of mathematical content and developmentally appropriate pedagogical knowledge to provide students with experiences that help them learn mathematics with understanding, while they reason about and make sense of the ideas that they encounter.

In 2010 the National Council of Teachers of Mathematics (NCTM) published the first book in the Essential Understanding Series, focusing on topics that are critical to the mathematical development of students but often difficult to teach. Written to deepen teachers' understanding of key mathematical ideas and to examine those ideas in multiple ways, the Essential Understanding Series was designed to fill in gaps and extend teachers' understanding by providing a detailed survey of the big ideas and the essential understandings related to particular topics in mathematics.

The Putting Essential Understanding into Practice Series builds on the Essential Understanding Series by extending the focus to classroom practice. These books center on the pedagogical knowledge that teachers must have to help students master the big ideas and essential understandings at developmentally appropriate levels.

To help students develop deeper understanding, teachers must have skills that go beyond knowledge of content. The authors demonstrate that for teachers–

- understanding student misconceptions is critical and helps in planning instruction;

- knowing the mathematical content is not enough–understanding student learning and knowing different ways of teaching a topic are indispensable;

- constructing a task is important because the way in which a task is constructed can aid in mediating or negotiating student misconceptions by providing opportunities to identify those misconceptions and determine how to address them.

Through detailed analysis of samples of student work, emphasis on the need to understand student thinking, suggestions for follow-up tasks with the potential to move students forward, and ideas for assessment, the Putting Essential Understanding into Practice Series demonstrates best practice for developing students' understanding of mathematics.

The ideas and understandings that the Putting Essential Understanding into Practice Series highlights for student mastery are also embodied in the Common Core State

Standards for Mathematics, and connections with these new standards are noted throughout each book.

On behalf of the Board of Directors of NCTM, I offer sincere thanks to everyone who has helped to make this new series possible. Special thanks go to Barbara J. Dougherty for her leadership as series editor and to all the authors for their work on the Putting Essential Understanding into Practice Series. I join the project team in welcoming you to this special series and extending best wishes for your ongoing enjoyment—and for the continuing benefits for you and your students—as you explore Putting Essential Understanding into Practice!

Linda M. Gojak
President, 2012–2014
National Council of Teachers of Mathematics

Preface

The Putting Essential Understanding into Practice Series explores the teaching of mathematics topics in grades K–12 that are difficult to learn and to teach. Each volume in this series focuses on specific content from one volume in NCTM's Essential Understanding Series and links it to ways in which those ideas can be taught successfully in the classroom.

Thus, this series builds on the earlier series, which aimed to present the mathematics that teachers need to know and understand well to teach challenging topics successfully to their students. Each of the earlier books identified and examined the big ideas related to the topic, as well as the "essential understandings"–the associated smaller, and often more concrete, concepts that compose each big idea.

Taking the next step, the Putting Essential Understanding into Practice Series shifts the focus to the specialized pedagogical knowledge that teachers need to teach those big ideas and essential understandings effectively in their classrooms. The Introduction to each volume details the nature of the complex, substantive knowledge that is the focus of these books–*pedagogical content knowledge*. For the topics explored in these books, this knowledge is both student centered and focused on teaching mathematics through problem solving.

Each book then puts big ideas and essential understandings related to the topic under a high-powered teaching lens, showing in fine detail how they might be presented, developed, and assessed in the classroom. Specific tasks, classroom vignettes, and samples of student work serve to illustrate possible ways of introducing students to the ideas in ways that will enable students not only to make sense of them now but also to build on them in the future. Items for readers' reflection appear throughout and offer teachers additional opportunities for professional development.

The final chapter of each book looks at earlier and later instruction on the topic. A look back highlights effective teaching that lays the earlier foundations that students are expected to bring to the current grades, where they solidify and build on previous learning. A look ahead reveals how high-quality teaching can expand students' understanding when they move to more advanced levels.

Each volume in the Putting Essential Understanding into Practice Series also includes three appendixes to extend and enrich readers' experiences and possibilities for using the book. The appendixes list the big ideas and essential understandings related to the topic, detail resources for teachers, and present tasks discussed in the book. These materials are also available to readers online at the More4U website, where Appendix 3 includes additional tasks, with templates to facilitate hands-on work with students. Readers can gain online access to each book's More4U materials by going to www.nctm.org/more4u and entering the code that appears on the title page. They can then print out these materials for personal or classroom use.

Because the topics chosen for both the earlier Essential Understanding Series and this successor series represent areas of mathematics that are widely regarded as challenging to teach and to learn, we believe that these books fill a tangible need for teachers. We hope that as you move through the tasks and consider the associated classroom implementations, you will find a variety of ideas to support your teaching and your students' learning.

Acknowledgments

We would like to thank the following teachers for implementing the material for this volume: Maria Griffith, David Jaeger, Kelsie Rites, Ruth Schnauble, Kati Stauder, Zac Stavish, and Alexandra Weyforth. We would also like to thank Serena Lee, Jocie Janowich, and Allison Young for sharing their thinking with us in interviews.

Introduction

Shulman (1986, 1987) identified seven knowledge bases that influence teaching:

1. Content knowledge

2. General pedagogical knowledge

3. Curriculum knowledge

4. Knowledge of learners and their characteristics

5. Knowledge of educational contexts

6. Knowledge of educational ends, purposes, and values

7. Pedagogical content knowledge

The specialized content knowledge that you use to transform your understanding of mathematics content into ways of teaching is what Shulman identified as item 7 on this list—*pedagogical content knowledge* (Shulman 1986). This is the knowledge that is the focus of this book—and all the volumes in the Putting Essential Understanding into Practice Series.

Pedagogical Content Knowledge

In mathematics teaching, pedagogical content knowledge includes at least four indispensable components:

1. Knowledge of curriculum for mathematics

2. Knowledge of assessments for mathematics

3. Knowledge of instructional strategies for mathematics

4. Knowledge of student understanding of mathematics (Magnusson, Krajcik, and Borko 1999)

These four components are linked in significant ways to the content that you teach.

Even though it is important for you to consider how to structure lessons, deciding what group and class management techniques you will use, how you will allocate time, and what will be the general flow of the lesson, Shulman (1986) noted that it is even more important to consider *what* is taught and the *way* in which it is taught. Every day, you make at least five essential decisions as you determine—

1. which explanations to offer (or not);

2. which representations of the mathematics to use;

3. what types of questions to ask;

4. what depth to expect in responses from students to the questions posed; and

5. how to deal with students' misunderstandings when these become evident in their responses.

Your pedagogical content knowledge is the unique blending of your content expertise and your skill in pedagogy to create a knowledge base that allows you to make robust instructional decisions. Shulman (1986, p. 9) defined pedagogical content knowledge as "a second kind of content knowledge…, which goes beyond knowledge of the subject matter per se to the dimension of subject matter knowledge *for teaching*." He explained further:

> Pedagogical content knowledge also includes an understanding of what makes the learning of specific topics easy or difficult: the conceptions and preconceptions that students of different ages and backgrounds bring with them to the learning of those most frequently taught topics and lessons. (p. 9)

If you consider the five decision areas identified at the top of the page, you will note that each of these requires knowledge of the mathematical content and the associated pedagogy. For example, teaching addition and subtraction requires that you understand the properties of the operations and then determine contextual situations that best embody those properties to present to your students. Your knowledge of addition and subtraction can help you craft tasks and questions that provide counterexamples and ways to guide your students in seeing connections across multiple number systems. As you establish the content, complete with learning goals, you then need to consider how to move your students from their initial understandings to deeper ones, building rich connections along the way.

The instructional sequence that you design to meet student learning goals has to take into consideration the misconceptions and misunderstandings that you might expect to encounter (along with the strategies that you expect to use to negotiate them), your expectation of the level of difficulty of the topic for your students, the progression of experiences in which your students will engage, appropriate collections of representations for the content, and relationships between and among addition and subtraction and other topics.

Model of Teacher Knowledge

Grossman (1990) extended Shulman's ideas to create a model of teacher knowledge with four domains (see fig. 0.1):

1. Subject-matter knowledge

2. General pedagogical knowledge

3. Pedagogical content knowledge

4. Knowledge of context

Subject-matter knowledge includes mathematical facts, concepts, rules, and relationships among concepts. Your understanding of the mathematics affects the way in which you teach the content—the ideas that you emphasize, the ones that you do not, particular algorithms that you use, and so on (Hill, Rowan, and Ball 2005).

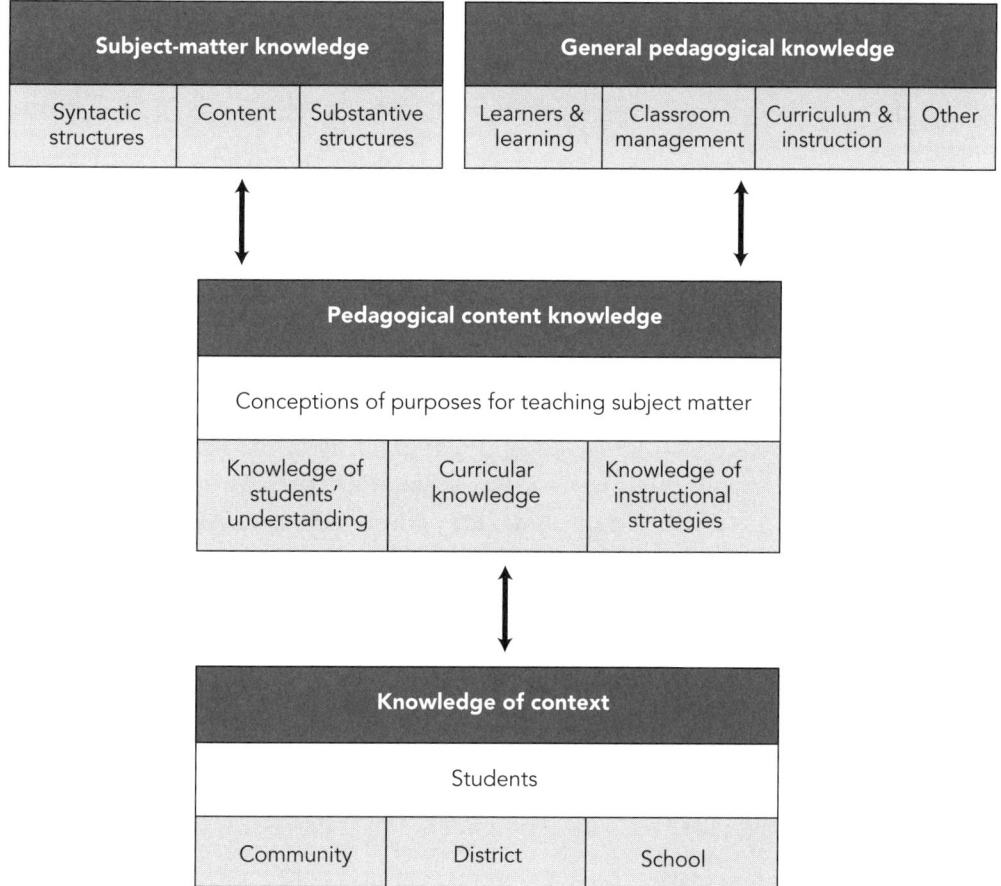

Fig. 0.1. Grossman's (1990, p. 5) model of teacher knowledge

Your pedagogical knowledge relates to the general knowledge, beliefs, and skills that you possess about instructional practices. These include specific instructional strategies that you use, the amount of wait time that you allow for students' responses to questions or tasks, classroom management techniques that you use for setting expectations and organizing students, and your grouping techniques, which might include having your students work individually or cooperatively or collaboratively, in groups or pairs. As Grossman's model indicates, your understanding and interpretation of the environment of your school, district, and community can also have an impact on the way in which you teach a topic.

Note that pedagogical content knowledge has four aspects, or components, in Grossman's (1990) model:

1. Conceptions of purposes for teaching

2. Knowledge of students' understanding

3. Knowledge of curriculum

4. Knowledge of instructional strategies

Each of these components has specific connections to the classroom. It is useful to consider each one in turn.

First, when you think about the goals that you want to establish for your instruction, you are focusing on your conceptions of the purposes for teaching. This is a broad category but an important one because the goals that you set will define learning outcomes for your students. These conceptions influence the other three components of pedagogical content knowledge. Hence, they appropriately occupy their overarching position in the model.

Second, your knowledge of your students' understanding of the mathematics content is central to good teaching. To know what your students understand, you must focus on both their conceptions and their misconceptions. As teachers, we all recognize that students develop naïve understandings that may or may not be immediately evident to us in their work or discourse. These can become deep-rooted misconceptions that are not simply errors that students make. Misconceptions may include incorrect generalizations that students have developed, such as the idea that addition "makes numbers bigger" and subtraction "makes numbers smaller." These generalizations may even be predictable notions that students exhibit as part of a developmental trajectory, such as thinking that subtraction is always "taking away."

Part of your responsibility as a teacher is to present tasks or to ask questions that can bring misconceptions to the forefront. Once you become aware of misconceptions in students' thinking, you then have to determine the next instructional steps. The mathematical ideas presented in this volume focus on common misconceptions that students form in relation to a specific topic—addition and subtraction. This book shows how the type of task selected and the sequencing of carefully developed questions can bring the misconceptions to light, as well as how particular teachers took the next instructional steps to challenge their students' misconceptions.

Third, curricular knowledge for mathematics includes multiple areas. Your teaching may be guided by a set of standards such as the Common Core State Standards for Mathematics (CCSSM; National Governors' Association Center for Best Practices and Council of Chief State School Officers 2010) or other provincial, state, or local standards. You may in fact use these standards as the learning outcomes for your students. Your textbook is another source that may influence your instruction. With any textbook also comes a particular philosophical view of mathematics, mathematics teaching, and student learning. Your awareness and understanding of the curricular perspectives related to the choice of standards and the selection of a textbook can help to determine how you actually enact your curriculum. Moreover, your district or school may have a pacing guide that influences your delivery of the curriculum. In this book, we can focus only on the alignment of the topics presented with broader curricular perspectives, such as CCSSM. However, your own understanding of and expertise with your other curricular resources, coupled with the parameters defined by the expected student outcomes from standards documents, can provide the specificity that you need for your classroom.

In addition to your day-to-day instructional decisions, you make daily decisions about which tasks from curricular materials you can use without adaptation, which tasks you will need to adapt, and which tasks you will need to create on your own. Once you select or develop meaningful, high-quality tasks and use them in your mathematics lesson, you have launched what Yinger (1988) called "a three-way conversation between teacher, student, and problem" (p. 86). This process is not simple—it is complex because how students respond to the problem or task is directly linked to your next instructional move. That means that you have to plan multiple instructional paths to choose among as students respond to those tasks.

Knowledge of the curriculum goes beyond the curricular materials that you use. You also consider the mathematical knowledge that students bring with them from pre-kindergarten and what they should learn by the end of grade 2. The way in which you teach a foundational concept or skill has an impact on the way in which students will interact with and learn later related content. For example, the types of representations that you include in your introduction of addition and subtraction are the ones that your students will use to evaluate other representations and ideas in later grades.

Fourth, knowledge of instructional strategies is essential to pedagogical content knowledge. Having a wide array of instructional strategies for teaching mathematics is central to effective teaching and learning. Instructional strategies, along with knowledge of the curriculum, may include the selection of mathematical tasks, together with the way in which those tasks will be enacted in the classroom. Instructional strategies may also include the way in which the mathematical content will be structured for students. You may have very specific ways of thinking about how you will structure your presentation of a mathematical idea—not only how you will sequence the introduction and development of the idea, but also how you will present that idea to your students. Which examples should you select, and which questions should you ask? What representations should you use? Your knowledge of instructional strategies, coupled with your knowledge of your curriculum, permits you to align the selected mathematical tasks closely with the way in which your students perform those tasks in your classroom.

The instructional approach in this volume combines a student-centered perspective with an approach to mathematics through problem solving. A student-centered approach is characterized by a shared focus on student and teacher conversations, including interactions among students. Students who learn through such an approach are active in the learning process and develop ways of evaluating their own work and one another's in concert with the teacher's evaluation.

Teaching through problem solving makes tasks or problems the core of mathematics teaching and learning. The introduction to a new topic consists of a task that students work through, drawing on their previous knowledge while connecting it with new ideas. After students have explored the introductory task (or tasks), their consideration of solution methods, the uniqueness or multiplicity of solutions, and extensions of the task create rich opportunities for discussion and the development of specific mathematical concepts and skills.

By combining the two approaches, teachers create a dynamic, interactive, and engaging classroom environment for their students. This type of environment promotes the ability of students to demonstrate CCSSM's Standards for Mathematical Practice while learning the mathematics at a deep level.

The chapters that follow will show that instructional sequences embed all the characteristics of knowledge of instructional strategies that Grossman (1990) identifies. One component that is not explicit in Grossman's model but is included in a model developed by Magnusson, Krajcik, and Borko (1999) is the knowledge of assessment. Your knowledge of assessment in mathematics plays an important role in guiding your instructional decision-making process.

There are different types of assessments, each of which can influence the evidence that you collect as well as your view of what students know (or don't know) and how they know what they do. Your interpretation of what students know is also related to your view of what constitutes "knowing" in mathematics. As you examine the tasks, classroom vignettes, and samples of student work in this volume, you will notice that teacher questioning permits formative assessment that supplies information that spans both conceptual and procedural aspects of understanding. *Formative assessment*, as this book uses the term, refers to an appraisal that occurs during an instructional segment, with the aim of adjusting instruction to meet the needs of students more effectively (Popham 2006). Formative assessment does not always require a paper-and-pencil product but may include questions that you ask or tasks that students complete during class.

The information that you gain from student responses can provide you with feedback that guides the instructional flow, while giving you a sense of how deeply (or superficially) your students understand a particular idea—or whether they hold a misconception that is blocking their progress. As you monitor your students' development of rich understanding, you can continually compare their responses with your expectations and then adapt your instructional plans to accommodate their current levels of development. Wiliam (2007, p. 1054) described this interaction between teacher expectations and student performance in the following way:

> It is therefore about assessment functioning as a bridge between teaching and learning, helping teachers collect evidence about student achievement in order to adjust instruction to better meet student learning needs, in real time.

Wiliam notes that for teachers to get the best information about student understandings, they have to know how to facilitate substantive class discussions, choose tasks that include opportunities for students to demonstrate their learning, and employ robust and effective questioning strategies. From these strategies, you must then interpret student responses and scaffold their learning to help them progress to more complex ideas.

Characteristics of Tasks

The type of task that is presented to students is very important. Tasks that focus only on procedural aspects may not help students learn a mathematical idea deeply.

Superficial learning may result in students forgetting easily, requiring reteaching, and potentially affecting how they understand mathematical ideas that they encounter in the future. Thus, the tasks selected for inclusion in this volume emphasize deep learning of significant mathematical ideas. These rich, "high-quality" tasks have the power to create a foundation for more sophisticated ideas and support an understanding that goes beyond "how" to "why." Figure 0.2 identifies the characteristics of a high-quality task.

As you move through this volume, you will notice that it sequences tasks for each mathematical idea so that they provide a cohesive and connected approach to the identified concept. The tasks build on one another to ensure that each student's thinking becomes increasingly sophisticated, progressing from a novice's view of the content to a perspective that is closer to that of an expert. We hope that you will find the tasks useful in your own classes.

A high–quality task has the following characteristics:
Aligns with relevant mathematics content standard(s)
Encourages the use of multiple representations
Provides opportunities for students to develop and demonstrate the mathematical practices
Involves students in an inquiry-oriented or exploratory approach
Allows entry to the mathematics at a low level (all students can begin the task) but also has a high ceiling (some students can extend the activity to higher-level activities)
Connects previous knowledge to new learning
Allows for multiple solution approaches and strategies
Engages students in explaining the meaning of the result
Includes a relevant and interesting context

Fig. 0.2. Characteristics of a high-quality task

Types of Questions

The questions that you pose to your students in conjunction with a high-quality task may at times cause them to confront ideas that are at variance with or directly contradictory to their own beliefs. The state of mind that students then find themselves in is called *cognitive dissonance,* which is not a comfortable state for students—or, on occasion, for the teacher. The tasks in this book are structured in a way that forces students to deal with two conflicting ideas. However, it is through the process of negotiating the contradictions that students come to know the content much more deeply. How the teacher handles this negotiation determines student learning.

You can pose three types of questions to support your students' process of working with and sorting out conflicting ideas. These questions are characterized by their potential to encourage reversibility, flexibility, and generalization in students' thinking (Dougherty 2001). All three types of questions require more than a one-word or one-number answer. Reversibility questions are those that have the capacity to change the direction of students' thinking. They often give students the solution and require them to create the corresponding problem. A flexibility question can be one of two types: it can ask students to solve a problem in more than one way, or it can ask them to compare and contrast two or more problems or determine the relationship between or among concepts and skills. Generalization questions also come in two types: they ask students to look at multiple examples or cases and find a pattern or make observations, or they ask them to create a specific example of a rule, conjecture, or pattern. Figure 0.3 provides examples of reversibility, flexibility, and generalization questions related to addition and subtraction.

Type of question	Example
Reversibility question	Find two numbers whose sum is 12. Find three more pairs of numbers with the numbers in each pair adding to 12.
Flexibility question	Compute 34 – 18. Perform the same subtraction in a different way.
Flexibility question	Compute the following: 53 + 68 55 + 70 58 + 63 How are these addition problems related?
Generalization question	What would you expect to be the maximum number of digits in the sum of two two-digit numbers?
Generalization question	Find two two-digit numbers that give a difference of one digit when one number is subtracted from the other.

Fig. 0.3. Examples of reversibility, flexibility, and generalization questions

Conclusion

The Introduction has provided a brief overview of the nature of—and necessity for—pedagogical content knowledge. This knowledge, which you use in your classroom every day, is the indispensable medium through which you transmit your understanding of the big ideas of the mathematics to your students. It determines your selection of appropriate, high-quality tasks and enables you to ask the types of questions that will not only move your students forward in their understanding but also allow you to determine the depth of that understanding.

The chapters that follow describe important ideas related to learners, curricular goals, instructional strategies, and assessment that can assist you in transforming your students' knowledge into formal mathematical ideas related to addition and subtraction. These chapters provide specific examples of mathematical tasks and student thinking for you to analyze to develop your pedagogical content knowledge for teaching addition and subtraction in prekindergarten–grade 2 or to give you ideas to help other colleagues develop this knowledge. You will also see how to bring together and interweave your knowledge of learners, curriculum, instructional strategies, and assessment to support your students in grasping the big ideas and essential understandings and using them to build more sophisticated knowledge.

Students entering prekindergarten have already had some experiences that affect their initial understanding of addition and subtraction. Furthermore, they have developed some ideas about these operations in other number contexts. Students in the first years of school frequently demonstrate understanding of mathematical ideas related to addition and subtraction in a particular context or in connection with a specific picture or drawing. Yet, in other situations, the same students do not demonstrate that same understanding. As their teacher, you must understand the ideas that they have developed about addition and subtraction in their prior experiences so you can extend this knowledge and see whether or how it differs from the formal mathematical knowledge that they need to be successful in reasoning with or applying addition and subtraction. You have the important responsibility of assessing their current knowledge related to the big ideas of addition and subtraction as well as their understanding of various representations of these operations and their power and limitations. Your understanding will facilitate and reinforce your instructional decisions. Teaching the big mathematical ideas and helping students develop essential understandings related to addition and subtraction is obviously a very challenging and complex task.

into practice

Chapter 1
Counting and Part-Part-Whole Relationships

Big Idea 1
Addition and subtraction are used to represent and solve many different kinds of problems.

Essential Understanding 1*a*
Addition and subtraction of whole numbers are based on sequential counting with whole numbers.

Essential Understanding 1*c*
Many different problem situations can be represented by part-part-whole relationships and addition or subtraction.

Essential Understanding 1*d*
Part-part-whole relationships can be expressed by using number sentences like $a + b = c$ or $c - b = a$, where a and b are the parts and c is the whole.

Developing Essential Understanding of Addition and Subtraction for Teaching Mathematics in Prekindergarten–Grade 2 (Caldwell, Karp, and Bay-Williams 2011) presents big ideas and essential understandings that teachers need to know well to teach addition and subtraction to students in prekindergarten–grade 2. A very natural way to begin putting this knowledge into practice in the classroom is by focusing on children's early development of number sense for addition and subtraction and the importance of providing young students with a multitude of experiences to compose and decompose number. Building understanding of part-part-whole relationships is central because this understanding is the cornerstone of addition and subtraction concepts, properties, and algorithms.

Common Core State Standards for Mathematics

Related to the Big Idea and Essential Understandings for Chapter 1

Kindergarten (K.OA.1–5)

1. Represent addition and subtraction with objects, fingers, mental images, drawings, sounds (e.g., claps), acting out situations, verbal explanations, expressions, or equations.

2. Solve addition and subtraction word problems, and add and subtract within 10, e.g., by using objects or drawings to represent the problem.

3. Decompose numbers less than or equal to 10 into pairs in more than one way, e.g., by using objects or drawings, and record each decomposition by a drawing or equation (e.g., $5 = 2 + 3$ and $5 = 4 + 1$).

4. For any number from 1 to 9, find the number that makes 10 when added to the given number, e.g., by using objects or drawings, and record the answer with a drawing or equation.

5. Fluently add and subtract within 5.

(National Governors Association Center for Best Practices and Council of Chief State School Officers [NGA Center and CCSSO] 2010, p. 11)

We cannot overstate the importance of these early experiences to students, whose understanding develops through these opportunities to represent their thinking and understanding. These experiences help them meet the expectations of the Common Core State Standards for Mathematics (CCSSM; NGA Center and CCSSO 2010), which detail outcomes for students' understanding of addition and subtraction, beginning in kindergarten and continuing into the elementary grades.

Counting as a Foundation for Addition and Subtraction

Acquiring fundamental counting skills is the hallmark of early number development for preschool and kindergarten students. These skills are critical to their acquisition of skills in addition and subtraction. Students need to have experiences to build four fundamental aspects of early numerical knowledge as they work toward the idea of an operation (Clements and Sarama 2014):

1. Number sequence

2. One-to-one correspondence

3. Cardinality

4. Subitizing

Students must have many opportunities to count objects of varying sizes and quantities so that they can develop competencies in these four areas. Students should engage in multiple activities that have the same basic form.

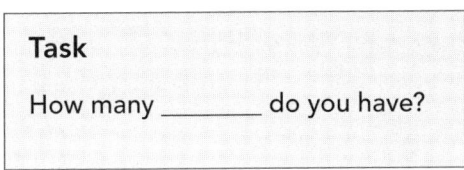

Task

How many _____ do you have?

Through such experiences, students develop a foundation for understanding and giving meaning to number and number relationships. The contexts for these situations influence how they count and what strategies they use to find the whole, or total quantity. These activities include tasks that focus on knowledge of the physical world (physical knowledge activities [Kamii and Rummelsburg 2008]).

One way to link counting with the idea of finding the whole amount is to conduct classroom inventories. You can send children, armed with clipboards, sticky notes, and pencils, off to different corners of the room to count and record numbers of blocks, books, crayons, and so on. Young children find counting a powerful experience and are eager to share their results. These experiences develop their understanding of cardinality and one-to-one correspondence between objects and numbers.

You can build interesting discussions on these counting adventures by asking different pairs of students to count the same objects and report their results. Having young students reconcile differences in the counts—that one pair counted 23 crayons and another pair counted 25 crayons—offers a powerful opportunity for them to develop the concept of accuracy while putting into practice standard 3 in the Standards for Mathematical Practice in the Common Core State Standards for Mathematics: "Construct viable arguments and critique the reasoning of others" (NGA Center and CCSSO 2010, p. 6).

You might also ask each pair to demonstrate their counting techniques for the class. After they have counted, you could ask them to share how they know when they have already counted an object. When young students demonstrate a simple technique such as moving an object to the side as it is counted, they help other students understand that this physical action is a crucial step in developing accuracy while promoting an understanding of one-to-one correspondence. Through multiple experiences, children sharpen their counting skills to include rote counting, one-to-one correspondence, conservation, accuracy, and understanding of magnitude. All of these understandings support their development of a sense of the meaning of the operations of addition and subtraction.

Another way of developing these foundational counting opportunities for children begins with reading counting books aloud to them. Counting books have been written on almost every imaginable topic and can be connected with many curricular areas and units. Figure 1.1 shows the work of kindergarten students who were given a contextualized counting activity after listening to the children's book *Counting in the Garden* (Parker 2005). The students were assigned to groups, and each was given a bag of garden items to inventory. Each group's bag had different numbers of particular items and different total amounts. Group members could decide to sort and count the items in their own way, but they had to figure out how to represent and report to the rest of the class what was in their bag.

Fig. 1.1. Two students' inventories of garden items

Students can enjoy very natural conversations about numbers while counting and comparing the contents of their bags. The following conversation occurred among students in two groups as the students discussed the objects in their inventoried bags. Maria and Marcus were in one group, and Selena and Tavon were in the other.

Maria: [*To Selena*] Our bag has only three butterflies! How many do you and Tavon have?

Tavon: We have five butterflies!

Marcus:	Awwww...
Tavon:	Yes, we have more!
Selena:	It's OK! If you and Maria had two more butterflies, then we would have the same!
Maria:	Yay! And besides, I think we have more yellow flowers than you.
Tavon:	Oh! How many do you have? Let's count 'em to find out.

This conversation illustrates the way in which young children build additive number relationships naturally by counting items and combining and comparing the numbers of objects that they have—in this case, the contents of their bags. You can facilitate small- and large-group discussions by encouraging your students to share their counting techniques, asking them to total their combinations of inventoried items, and inviting them to compare different numbers of items. Questions like the following encourage this thinking:

- "How did you organize your items?"

- "Why did you organize your items that way?"

- "What item do you have the greatest number of in your bag?"

- "What item do you have the smallest number of in your bag?"

- "Who has the same number of [*particular items*] as [*a particular student*]?"

- "Who has more [*particular items*] than [*a particular student*]? How many more?"

- "Who has fewer [*particular items*] than [*a particular student*]? How many fewer?"

- "How many items do you and [*a particular student*] have together?"

- "Does anyone have two more [*particular items*] than [*a particular student*]?"

Student misconceptions about number often arise from immature counting skills and difficulty in understanding number sequence, one-to-one correspondence, and number magnitude. Students vary greatly in their ability to count and record numbers of objects, but they can progress rapidly when given many rich experiences. Students also need to hear other students count aloud, have opportunities to compare their count of a collection of items with others' counts of the same collection, and then explore ways to reconcile differing totals. Reflect 1.1 invites you to consider ways of ensuring that *all* students have access to these types of opportunities.

Reflect 1.1

Activities that call for conducting inventories in the classroom can be differentiated for students with varying abilities.

How might you differentiate inventories for your students?

How might inventories address several of the common student misconceptions related to immature counting skills and difficulties in understanding number sequence, one-to-one correspondence, and number magnitude?

Many children's books promote counting skills and understanding of relationships among numbers. *The Icky Bug Counting Book* (Pallotta 1991) is a preschool and kindergarten favorite that can be connected easily and directly with a unit of study on insects. After reading the book aloud to your students, you can give them collections of plastic insects or pictures of insects to sort, count, combine, and compare, recording their results. Alternatively, if the technology is available, you might have your students create a collection of insects to count by giving them digital cameras and sending them off on a bug hunt to count, record, and then report their discoveries through number sentences. No matter how students obtain their collections, you can then engage them in a discussion of the numbers of different insects that they have counted and ask questions that will help them use their counting and recording to report their results.

You might also extend this approach to a more advanced counting book, *Counting Jennie* (Pittman 1994), which portrays a young girl who counts her way through the day with a constant stream of addition and subtraction problems, including problems with two-digit numbers.

The Bag I Am Taking to Grandma's (Neitzle 1986) is another children's book that offers rich possibilities for counting experiences. After reading the book to your students, you can have them create inventories of items that they might need for an overnight stay. Students can determine the objects and draw pictures of them inside an outline of an overnight bag (see fig. 1.2). They can then share their work and "read" one another's inventories and report the total quantity in each one. Depending on their level of understanding, students can differentiate the total value by quantity. They can create and record number sentences to represent the combined items in their bags or the difference between the numbers of items in their bags and a partner's.

Fig. 1.2. A student's record of what is in the suitcase

Understanding Relationships among Numbers

It is important for students to compare numbers and build their understanding of relationships among them. Reflect 1.2 asks you to predict how a young student might compare two particular one-digit numbers.

Reflect 1.2

How are 4 and 6 alike?

How would you expect a kindergarten or first–grade student to respond to this question?

What might the response tell you about the child's thinking about relationships between two numbers?

Interviews with first graders who were asked, "How are 4 and 6 alike?" offered insight into their thinking regarding relationships between numbers. Consider the following excerpts from interviews with three students—Sarita, Rema, and Jose— and then respond to the questions in Reflect 1.3.

Student 1: Sarita

Sarita: 4 and 6 are not alike, because 4 has straight lines in it, and 6 has a circle in it!

Student 2: Rema

Rema: I see 4 on my way to 6.

Teacher: What do you mean?

Rema: [*Stands up*] 1, 2, 3; hi, 4. Then there's 5 and 6.

Teacher: What was going on here?

Rema: I was walking on a number line, and I saw 4 on my way to 6.

Student 3: Jose

Jose: Well, 4 is part of 6.

Teacher: It is? How?

Jose: Well, if you have 6 things, then you have 4 things, of course. Actually, you have 4 things in all numbers bigger than 4.

Reflect 1.3

What do you notice about Sarita's, Rema's, and Jose's responses to the question, "How are 4 and 6 alike?"

Which responses reveal a naïve understanding of the relationship between the numbers? Why?

Which responses are more sophisticated? Why?

Students' misconceptions about relationships among numbers indicate the sophistication of their mathematical thinking. Students who focus on the formation of the numerals may not fully understand their values. To build understanding of relationships among numbers, students need to be able to represent quantities to compare.

Exploring "Both Addends Unknown"

Kindergartners can begin to think about problems of particular types. Several additive types are easier for them to interpret than others. One is rooted in situations with both addends unknown. Tasks that support students' understanding of this type of problem have a common form, with the blank filled in by a number up to 10.

Task

How many ways can you show _____ ?

Students' work with this task connects with and supports their understanding of relationships among numbers. At the same time, this work takes their understanding to the level of early algebraic thinking as the children find all the whole number combinations that yield a given total and justify that they have found all possibilities.

To develop flexible thinking about part-part-whole relationships, students need to understand that numbers can be represented in many ways. You should provide many opportunities for students to construct multiple representations of number values, using a variety of materials and a range of values. Initially, students should compose and decompose these values by using a given total so that they focus on the parts that create the same whole. If the total values are constantly changing within a lesson, students often completely fail to understand how the parts are composed to create the same whole and may develop misconceptions about how many ways they can represent a given value.

Also, if you encourage students to be systematic in their representations, you can help them develop an understanding of the patterns related to the combinations. After students have composed and decomposed many variations for a given value, they can discuss, compare, and share their results. Students are often amazed at the variety of number combinations that they and their classmates can create for a given quantity.

Another children's book, *Jack and the Beanstalk* (Kellogg 1997), presents an engaging context for a productive activity with two-sided (two-colored) counters or beans that have been spray-painted on one side. Building on this fairy-tale context, students can explore two-number combinations that yield a particular sum up to 10, given in the blank in the following task statement.

Task

If you toss _____ of Jack's beans, how many different ways can they land?

(Based on *Jack and the Beanstalk* [Kellogg 1997])

After students have tossed a particular number of Jack's beans multiple times, they can investigate and represent the two-color results. Initially, students can color in outlines of beans on paper and then progress to recording the values of the beans. Students should advance to larger quantities as they develop their understanding. Figure 1.3 shows student responses in vertically arranged progressions, from pictures to spoken words to written numerical symbols.

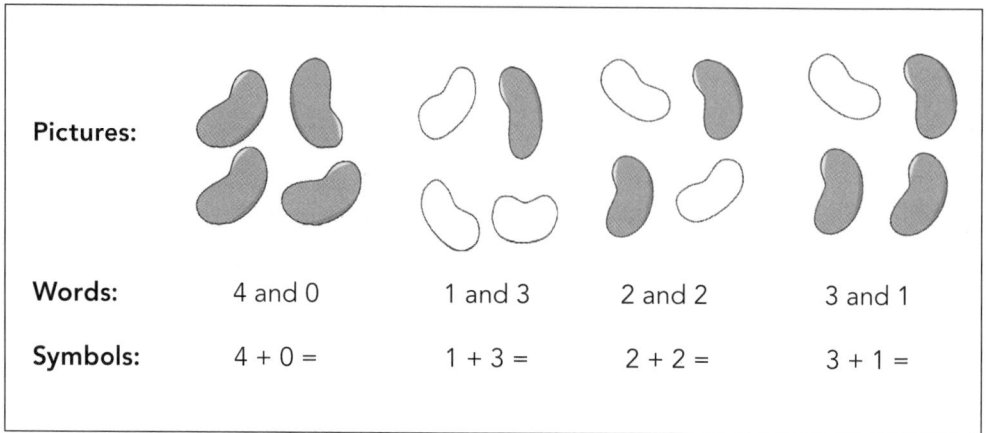

Pictures:				
Words:	4 and 0	1 and 3	2 and 2	3 and 1
Symbols:	4 + 0 =	1 + 3 =	2 + 2 =	3 + 1 =

Fig. 1.3. Progressions of student responses, from visual to oral to numerical records

The children's book *There Is a Carrot in My Ear and Other Noodle Tales* (Schwartz 1982) describes the escapades of the silly Noodle family. This book offers another context for an exploration of unknown addends, the Macaroni Squeeze game. To engage your students in this game, you will need uncooked, small noodles and several small, clear sandwich bags with self-sealing closures. Affix a piece of colored tape or draw a line with a permanent marker down the middle of each bag, as shown in figure 1.4a. An alternative, shown in figure 1.4b, is to draw a circle on the bag.

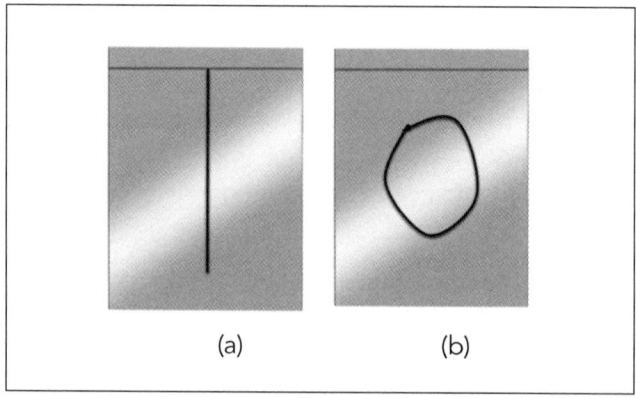

(a)   (b)

Fig. 1.4. Two options for preparing clear sandwich bags
for use in the Macaroni Squeeze game

Put 7 noodles (or another number of noodles, up to 10) in each clear plastic bag, and then seal it. Place the bags flat on a table or desk for your students to work with them on the task.

Task: Macaroni Squeeze

How many ways can you arrange the noodles in the bag?

Students move noodles to either side of the line (or in or out of the circle) and record their results. They can approach this task in a variety of ways, exploring different compositions of the given number of noodles. Observe how students find all the combinations. Do they use a random approach or a systematic strategy? As students find and record the different combinations, they can begin to understand that the whole remains constant while the parts change. Figure 1.5 shows different ways in which students might represent their work with 7 noodles.

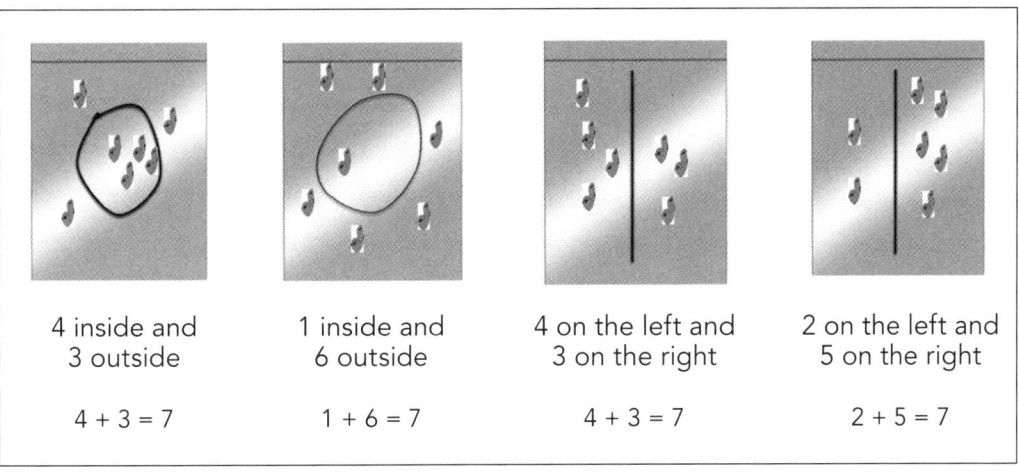

4 inside and 3 outside	1 inside and 6 outside	4 on the left and 3 on the right	2 on the left and 5 on the right
4 + 3 = 7	1 + 6 = 7	4 + 3 = 7	2 + 5 = 7

Fig. 1.5. Several ways in which students might represent arrangements of noodles

Another children's book that offers a motivating opportunity for exploring situations where both addends are unknown is *Guinea Pigs Add Up* (Cuyler 2010). This book tells the story of a classroom in which an active guinea pig population grows and decreases as babies are born and pets are distributed to interested adoptive families. This context presents an ideal situation for a variety of additive tasks; the following is one example.

Task: Where Are the Guinea Pigs?

There are 10 guinea pigs in 2 cages. Write equations to show how many guinea pigs are in each cage. How do you know that you have all the possible options?

(Based on *Guinea Pigs Add Up* [Cuyler 2010])

Start with two illustrations of cages (see fig. 1.6) serving as mats for your students to use in sorting counters (see fig. 1.7) to assign guinea pigs to cages. (Appendix 3 at More4U provides templates for cage mats and guinea pig counters for students' use in testing different arrangements of the guinea pigs in the cages.) Distribute the cage work mats and the guinea pig counters, and say to your students, "These 2 cages have 10 guinea pigs in all. Where are the guinea pigs?"

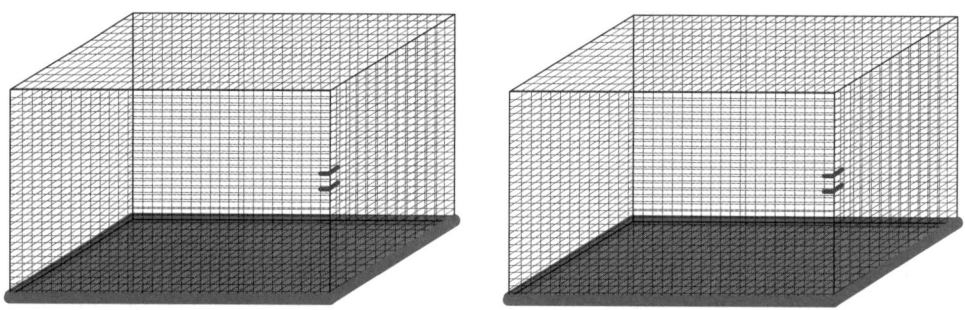

Fig. 1.6. Two cages; template for a student work mat available at More4U (Appendix 3)

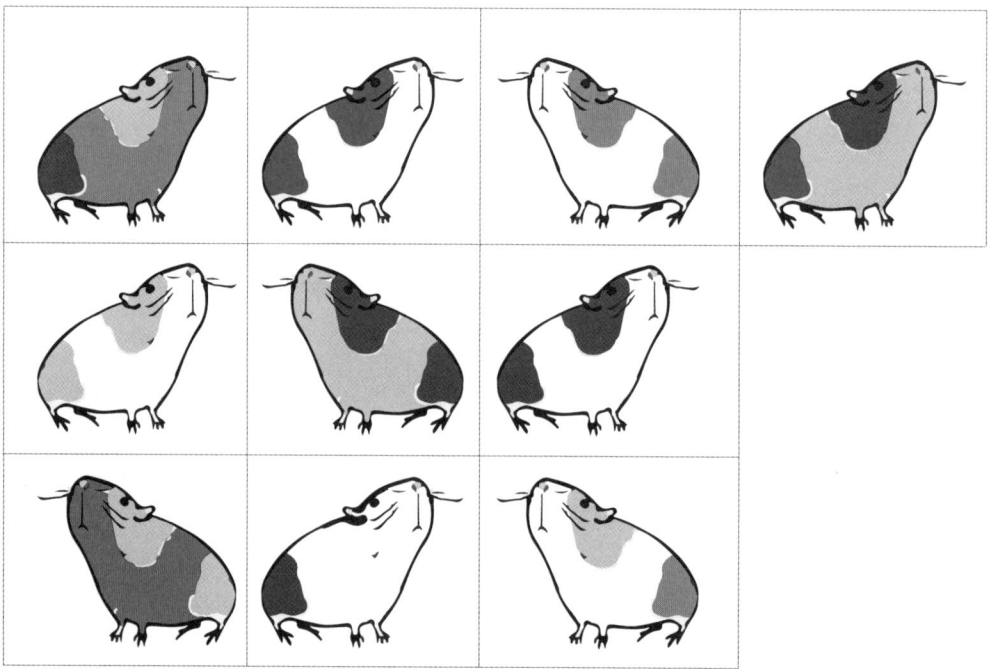

Fig. 1.7. Ten guinea pigs; template available in Appendix 3 at More4U

Figure 1.8 shows one student's work on the task; a link to a student's pencast (Livescribe file) is available at More4U. The task starts as a simple decomposition activity, supporting students' ability to "Decompose numbers less than or equal to 10 into pairs in more than one way" (NGA Center and CCSSO 2010, K.OA.3, p. 11). However, as students determine all possible options for showing 10, the task deepens, moving to offer an early experience in algebraic thinking. It also lends itself to use as a first step in exploring the structures of problems.

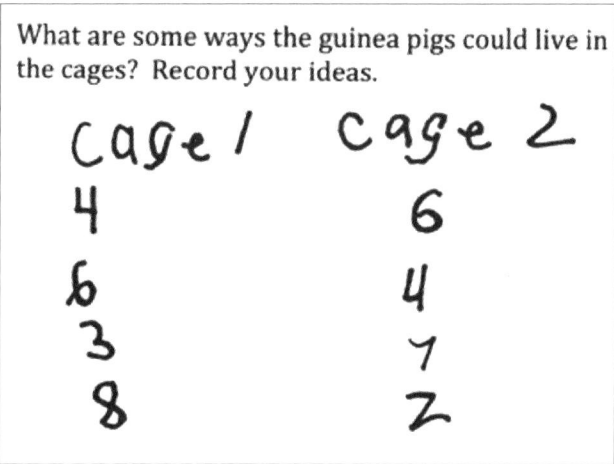

Fig. 1.8. A sample of student work on the task Where Are the Guinea Pigs?

Subitizing for Efficiency

Subitizing is naming a quantity without counting. It is a compelling counting strategy that supports an understanding of number. By developing your students' skills in subitizing, you can foster their understanding of cardinality (Benoit, Lehalle, and Jouen 2004). When students count objects one by one, over and over, they often focus on counting and making the one-to-one correspondence between each number and each object, but sometimes they do not make the transition to the principle of cardinality. By using subitizing as a tool, you can help your students learn that naming the quantity as they see it and then counting the parts to explain their thinking also names the whole set.

Subitizing also supports students' understanding of the part-whole relationship (Clements 1999) because students see the whole, but depending on the representation of objects or dots in use, they can decompose the parts in different ways. As students explore multiple representations of a number, subitizing helps them use spatial organization to visualize and instantly recognize quantities in many different arrangements, building flexibility in the way in which they think about number. Students can work with subitized values by using dot cards with varying numbers of dots and visual representations. In the classroom dialogue that follows, the teacher shows students the dot card that appears in figure 1.9 and asks them to name the total number of dots and then explain how they found their answer.

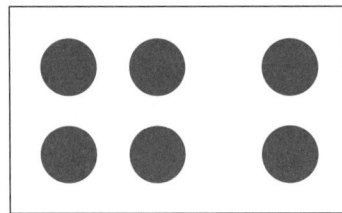

Fig. 1.9. A dot card used to develop students' skills in subitizing

Teacher: Can you name the number of dots that you see?

Allie: I see 6.

Teacher: Can you explain what you see?

Allie: I see 4, and then I counted, 5, 6.

Teacher: Did anyone else see it differently?

Roberto: I see 3 on the top row, and 3 on the bottom row makes 6.

To help your students think about the part-whole relationship, you can ask them to share the total number that they see by using the language of parts and wholes. Reflect 1.4 provides an opportunity to explore this idea in the context of the ten frame shown in figure 1.10.

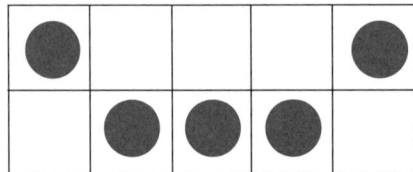

Fig. 1.10. A ten frame with counters

Reflect 1.4

Look at the ten frame in figure 1.10, and think about how you would describe what you see, using the language of parts and wholes.

Make a prediction about how students might interpret the ten frame.

Compare your prediction about students' interpretations of the ten frame with the responses of two students, Rita and Jenna, in the following classroom exchange:

Teacher:	Name and explain what you see.
Jenna:	I see 5! I see 2 on the top and 3 on the bottom!
Teacher:	What is the whole number of dots on this card?
Jenna:	5!
Teacher:	How do you know?
Jenna:	Because there are 5 dots!
Teacher:	What are the parts that you see, Jenna?
Jenna:	One of my parts is 2 and the other is 3.
Teacher:	Does anyone else see other parts?
Rita:	I see one of my parts as 1 and the other part as 4.
Teacher:	Can you explain that, Rita?
Rita:	I see 1 on the first box and then 4 more.
Teacher:	So what is your whole?
Rita:	5.
Teacher:	Wow, we talked about two ways to make 5 just by using this one ten-frame card.

Frequent use of subitizing is essential to developing this technique. Short, recurrent sessions along with powerful discussions using explicit vocabulary help students develop understanding of the part-part-whole relationships that they are seeing and increase their ability to retain the information that they are learning (Resnick 1983).

Often when students struggle in describing their thinking about subitizing, they just need more experience. Gradually, they become more able to describe what they see and how they see the values. Initially, some students may need to try smaller quantities and then ramp up. The children's book *10 Black Dots* (Crews 1995) can set the stage for a fruitful task. The student fills in the first blank with a number up to 10 and the second blank with the name of an object that has that many black dots.

Task: Picturing with Black Dots

_____ black dots can make a _____ . See my picture!

(Based on *10 Black Dots* [Crews 1995])

Students can create a picture by using a designated quantity of dots but breaking it into two parts or combining or comparing the dots in two different pictures. The whole class can create pages of black-dot pictures by using combinations that make the same quantity or different quantities. You can put a classroom book of the pages in a learning center and let students subitize one another's creations. Figure 1.11 shows two students' work on the Picturing with Black Dots task.

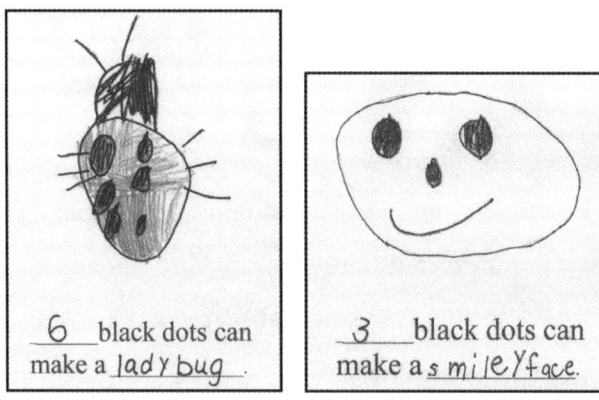

Fig. 1.11. Two sample pages for Picturing with Black Dots

Linking Contexts with Concrete Representations

Concrete representations are just one type among the variety of types of representations for additive problems. Yet, their value cannot be overemphasized. Whether students use beans, plastic counters, dot cards, ten frames, Rekenreks, Cuisenaire rods, part-whole graphic organizers, tape diagrams, or, eventually, number lines, they need to develop flexibility in using these representations. Some contexts lend themselves to concrete representations with particular tools. Consider the Rekenrek as an example.

The Rckenrek was developed by researchers in the Netherlands and consists of a rectangular frame supporting two wires strung with 10 beads apiece (see fig. 1.12). Each group of 10 beads is broken in the middle into two groups of 5, distinguished by color. This arrangement encourages students to see and think in groups of 5 or 10. In the classroom vignette that follows, a teacher is working with students with a Rekenrek.

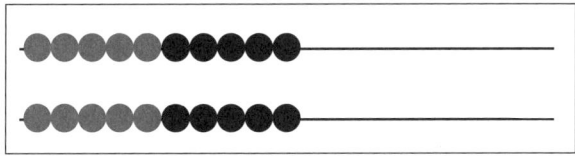

Fig. 1.12. A Rekenrek, or two-part bead frame

Teacher: I am thinking of a way to show 9 on my Rekenrek. Can you show me a way?

Students: Yes!

Amelia: I have 6 on the top and 3 on the bottom.

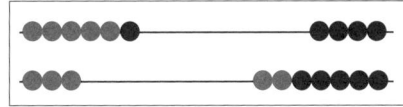

Teacher: [*Writing* 6 + 3 = 9 *on the board:*] Let's show Amelia's answer by writing it here.

Jocie: I have 8 on the top and 1 on the bottom!

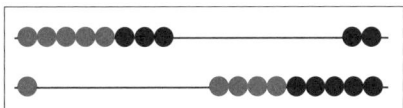

Teacher: So, Jocie, if the whole is 9, can you tell me what your two parts are?

Jocie: One of my parts is 8, and the other is 1.

Teacher: How can we write that as a number sentence?

Jocie: 8 + 1?

> *Teacher:* Let's write that down [*writes* 8 + 1 = 9 *on the board*]. Now, we have two ways to make 9. How many ways do you think we can find?

[*The teacher waits, letting the students think before speaking again.*]

> *Teacher:* Is there a way we could use Jocie's idea of 8 + 1 to help us find other combinations?

Many students begin with an unorganized list. If your students start in this manner, record their results in an organized list as they report them. Lead them in a discussion about any patterns that they notice, and then prompt a discussion about using logical thinking. When students move to making an organized list, the mere construction of such a list requires some sophistication in their thinking.

By noticing a pattern and recording the combinations as they discover the pattern, students can begin to develop their understanding of part-part-whole combinations. Students should watch a classmate model the development of the pattern by consciously moving one item at a time. When students make an unorganized listing, the combinations may remain mysterious and numerous (with some repeated at times) because they do not see the relationships of the parts to the whole, the power of the commutative property, or the structure of the part-part-whole model.

A number of contexts offer rich possibilities for use of the Rekenrek to link a context with a concrete representation. Some appealing contexts are available in children's literature. For example, you might read *Anno's Counting House* (Anno 1982) to your students and use a Rekenrek to represent a two-story house (or two stories in an apartment building if you have a book or plotline that links to that scenario). Link the two stories of the house to the two levels of the Rekenrek, as illustrated in figure 1.13. The number 8 in the peak of the house is the total number of people in the two-story house, with the Rekenrek representing 2 people downstairs and 6 people upstairs.

Other children's books also offer contexts that lend themselves to the use of a Rekenrek to reinforce the connection between context and concrete representation. This tool works well with storybook contexts involving bunk beds; books such as *How Many Feet in the Bed?* (Hamm 1994) and *The Napping House* (Wood 2009) can set the stage for this work. Also consider reading *The Memory Cupboard: A Thanksgiving Story* (Herman 2003) and using the Rekenrek to show the placement of different numbers of items on two shelves in a cabinet. Each of these stories presents a context that you can model nicely on the Rekenrek, double ten frames, or other two-part representational tools. (Another possibility is to visit the school library and create situations involving the placement of books on two shelves.)

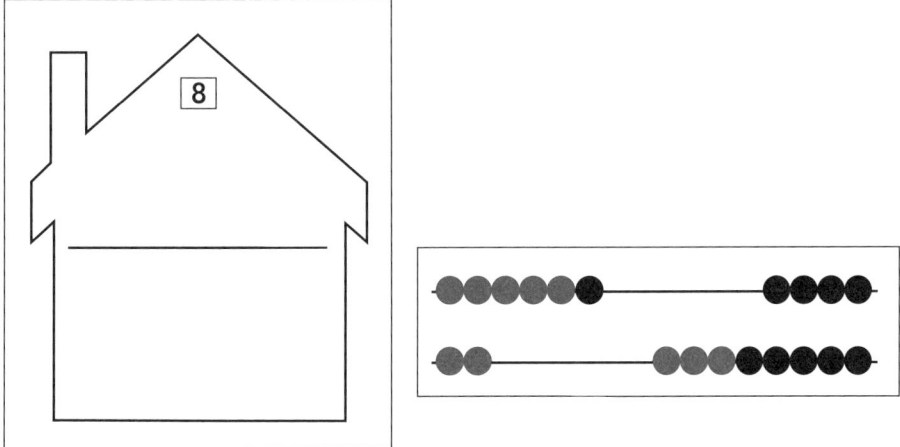

Fig. 1.13. Linking the context of *Anno's Counting House* with the concrete representation provided by the Rekenrek

Also be sure to link representations on the Rekenrek with part-part-whole situations as students use the color change in the beads to link a semi-concrete representation and an abstract representation in an equation. For example, ask, "If there are 10 people in the house, how many people are upstairs and how many people are downstairs?" Then ask the students to use the Rekenrek to show how many people might be upstairs and downstairs, recording their responses in number sentences.

The next section focuses on investigating missing addends. Reflect 1.5 leads into that discussion by probing the use of representations to build understanding of part-part-whole relationships.

Reflect 1.5

How might the use of multiple representations support student understanding of part–part–whole concepts?

What questions could you ask students to promote this understanding?

Investigating Missing Addends

After students have had multiple and varied opportunities to find parts for quantities and compare and explain the parts and wholes, they will be ready to make the transition to situations with a missing addend. You can build the concept of the missing addend by using the very same tools that you used to build their understanding of multiple representations of a number.

Consider the Hen and Egg game, for example. To play this game with your students, you will need beans or other counters to represent eggs and a cup or paper cutout of a chicken to represent a hen. Decide on a target number up to 10—say, 8—and place 8 beans, as eggs, on the desk (see fig. 1.14).

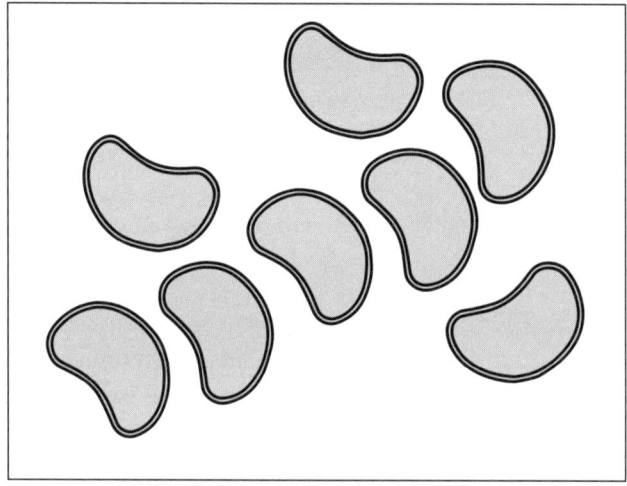

Fig. 1.14. Eight beans representing 8 eggs in the Hen and Egg game

After directing the students' attention to the 8 eggs, move the hen cutout to "sit on" some number of eggs, hiding them completely from view (see fig. 1.15). First say, "There are 8 eggs in the whole nest." Then ask, "How many eggs is the hen sitting on?" Relate the language of part-part-whole by saying to your students, "You know what one of the parts is, and you know what the whole is, but now you need to find the value of the missing part."

Ask the students to name the part and the whole and find the missing part. Students can play this game in pairs, with one student using the cup or hen cutout to hide some of the eggs and then asking the other student to name the missing part.

Dot cards like the sample shown in figure 1.16 also give students strong visual support for finding a missing addend when they know the whole and one of the parts. Filling in both blanks with the same number sets the task shown on the next page.

Fig 1.15. A "hen" "sitting on" some of the 8 "eggs" in the nest

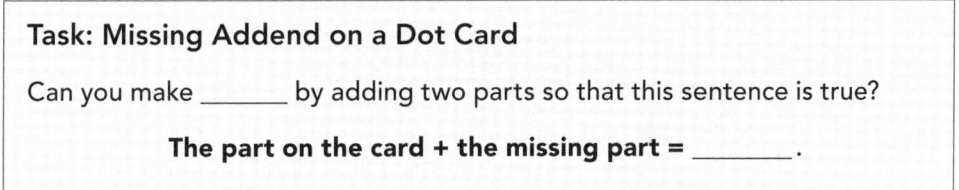

Task: Missing Addend on a Dot Card

Can you make _____ by adding two parts so that this sentence is true?

The part on the card + the missing part = _____.

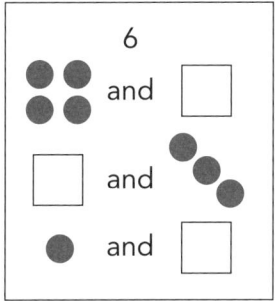

Fig. 1.16. A dot card showing a sample task

Students who are unable to find a missing part or give incorrect missing parts, or parts that do not match the total value, may have misconceptions about how to find a missing addend. Using smaller quantities or representing the missing parts with physical models can scaffold their thinking.

Another useful way to support students' exploration of missing parts is by playing a hiding game that comes very naturally to young students. Small children frequently clutch some small object, known only to them, in a closed fist. Find a number of small items, such as buttons or pennies, that you can easily hide in your hand. Show the whole collection to your students in your open hand (or state the total number) before closing your hand. (With very young children, have them count and place the counters in your hand.) Once students know the whole, carefully transfer some of the counters to your other hand, keeping them hidden from view. Then reveal the remaining part of the collection in your first hand, as shown in figure 1.17. Ask, "How many am I hiding in my other hand?" Start with very small quantities and gradually increase them. Students can state the missing part or represent it in front of them with different counters or cubes, matching what is in your hands. Once again, precise and explicit language on your part will help your students connect the representation with the part-part-whole language.

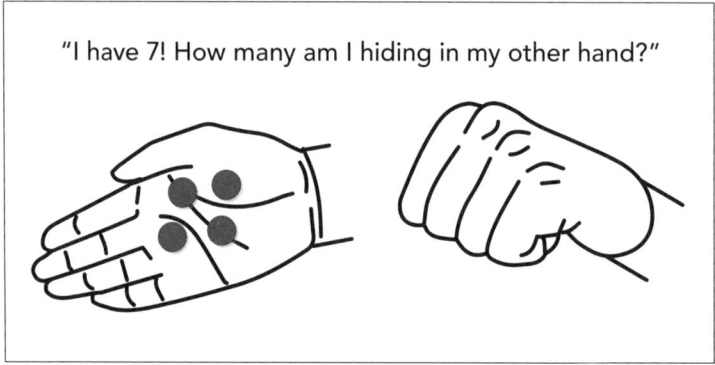

Fig. 1.17. An example of the hiding game

A number of children's books, including *A Pocket for Corduroy* (Freeman 1978), *Ten Apples on Top!* (Dr. Seuss 1961), *Caps for Sale* (Slobodkina 1940), and *Sheep in a Jeep* (Shaw 1986), can reinforce young learners' development of part-part-whole concepts. After reading the book aloud to your students, you can present part-part-whole tasks that engage them in finding missing parts. For example, the following task related to *A Pocket for Corduroy* asks students to explore a situation in which both addends are unknown; figure 1.18 shows a task card and a sample of student work.

Task: Corduroy's Pocket, Inside and Out

Corduroy has 8 pennies. Some are inside his pocket, and some are out. What could be inside his pocket?

(Based on *A Pocket for Corduroy* [Freeman 1978])

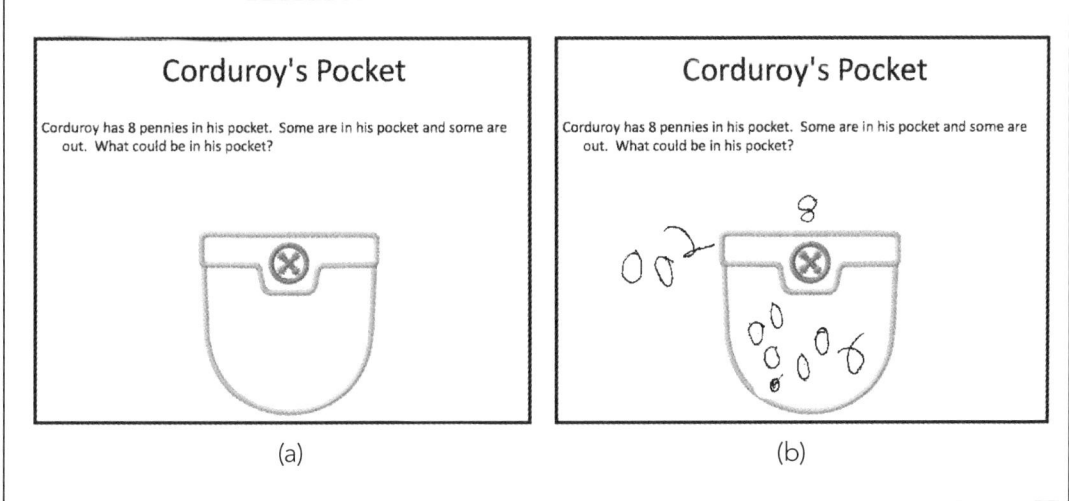

Fig. 1.18. Corduroy's Pocket, Inside and Out: (a) task card and (b) student work showing 2 + 6 = 8

Summary: Learners, Curriculum, Instruction, and Assessment

Teaching counting and part-part-whole concepts requires teachers to have an understanding of learners, curriculum, instruction, and assessment. Understanding learners helps in structuring meaningful tasks for them as they learn to count, compare, and determine part-part-whole relationships for given wholes. Sequencing and designing tasks is a significant component of implementing the curriculum. The associated instructional strategies should support students' construction of knowledge as they build their understanding of counting, parts and wholes, contexts linked to representations, and missing addends. These strategies include asking questions that scaffold students' progress to more complex ideas.

Assessing students' thinking throughout the process involves creating opportunities and investing time to probe their understanding as well as to uncover any misconceptions. You can examine how your students compose and decompose values, and how they find and record the parts for a given whole, to help you determine which quantities you might introduce next. You can evaluate whether your students use systematic ways to find all the parts for a whole or whether they rely on random or incomplete strategies. You can also assess your students' strategies for determining missing addends and then design tasks that support their thinking and understanding.

By consciously designing classroom tasks that integrate the four components—learners, curriculum, instructional strategies, and assessment—you can provide a full range of classroom experiences that will challenge and support all learners.

Conclusion

This chapter has discussed the importance of foundational counting experiences, rich tasks using literature, and questioning to promote a deep understanding of counting and part-part-whole relationships. Students need many opportunities to compose and decompose quantities to develop their understanding of the various ways to construct a whole and determine the relationship of parts to wholes. We have emphasized the importance of giving students many opportunities to count, record, and report inventories of many different types of objects, preparing them to progress to decomposing the whole into multiple parts. We have shared real conversations to illustrate student thinking about numbers to show how teachers and students engage in communicating about part-part-whole relationships. We have also included many examples of student work to demonstrate how students think about constructing parts and wholes within rich tasks. Students need a great variety of these experiences so that they can explore, discuss, and share their ideas. Although many of these experiences are open-ended, you should think carefully about the questions that you ask and the scaffolding that you provide so that your students can make important discoveries about how to compose and decompose given values.

practice

Chapter 2
Understanding Addition and Subtraction in Context

Big Idea 1
Addition and subtraction are used to represent and solve many different kinds of problems.

Essential Understanding 1*b*
Subtraction has an inverse relationship with addition.

Essential Understanding 1*c*
Many different problem situations can be represented by part-part-whole relationships and addition or subtraction.

Essential Understanding 1*d*
Part-part-whole relationships can be expressed by using number sentences like $a + b = c$ or $c - b = a$, where a and b are the parts and c is the whole.

Essential Understanding 1*e*
The context of a problem situation and its interpretation can lead to different representations.

In the past, when people thought about early elementary school mathematics, they might have said that it began with $2 + 2 = 4$. However, instruction in addition and subtraction should not begin with naked numbers such as those in that basic problem but instead should start with contextual problems. To give students a full understanding of additive situations in real-world contexts, instruction should emphasize the meaning of the operation embedded within a particular situation rather than launch a series of lessons with numerals alone. Focusing exclusively on numerical procedures does not support students' understanding of operations.

Common Core State Standards for Mathematics

Related to the Big Idea and Essential Understandings for Chapter 2

Kindergarten (K.OA.1–5)

1. Represent addition and subtraction with objects, fingers, mental images, drawings, sounds (e.g., claps), acting out situations, verbal explanations, expressions, or equations.

2. Solve addition and subtraction word problems, and add and subtract within 10, e.g., by using objects or drawings to represent the problem.

3. Decompose numbers less than or equal to 10 into pairs in more than one way, e.g., by using objects or drawings, and record each decomposition by a drawing or equation (e.g., $5 = 2 + 3$ and $5 = 4 + 1$).

4. For any number from 1 to 9, find the number that makes 10 when added to the given number, e.g., by using objects or drawings, and record the answer with a drawing or equation.

5. Fluently add and subtract within 5.

Grade 1 (1.OA.1–2)

1. Use addition and subtraction within 20 to solve word problems involving situations of adding to, taking from, putting together, taking apart, and comparing, with unknowns in all positions, e.g., by using objects, drawings, and equations with a symbol for the unknown number to represent the problem.

2. Solve word problems that call for addition of three whole numbers whose sum is less than or equal to 20, e.g., by using objects, drawings, and equations with a symbol for the unknown number to represent the problem.

Grade 2 (2.OA.1)

1. Use addition and subtraction within 100 to solve one- and two-step word problems involving situations of adding to, taking from, putting together, taking apart, and comparing, with unknowns in all positions, e.g., by using drawings and equations with a symbol for the unknown number to represent the problem.

(National Governors Association Center for Best Practices and Council of Chief State School Officers [NGA Center and CCSSO] 2010, pp. 11, 15, 19)

Students demonstrate many misunderstandings about when to add and when to subtract in contextual situations, especially when their first exposure to these operations has been with naked numbers. Furthermore, these difficulties are not restricted to young children who are first learning the operations—they persist for years. This chapter begins with an emphasis on the importance of having students consider addition and subtraction problems in a context. Doing so helps to teach children to apply their school learning immediately to real situations while they simultaneously make connections back to the experiences that they had before they began their formal schooling. But even when you plan your instruction and present contextualized tasks with good intentions, you will sometimes notice that your students approach these problems in a routine fashion, without engaging in the sense making or mindful use of strategies that you had anticipated. Children's initial methods are often not unlike the one described in this well-known quotation: "One learns to read the problem, to extract the relevant numbers and the operation to be used, to perform the operation, and to write down the result—without ever thinking about what it all means" (National Research Council 1990, p. 36).

According to reports of the National Assessment of Educational Progress (NAEP) over a period of more than twenty-five years, when children are asked to carry out basic computational problems, they are usually able to do so, yet their limited ability to understand basic mathematical concepts presented in word problems is one of the greatest weaknesses of U.S. students in mathematics (National Research Council 2001). Some recent data that we collected about student thinking related to word problems aligns with this finding.

We gave the infamous How Old Is the Shepherd problem (Merseth 1993) to 214 students in third, sixth, and seventh grades:

Task: How Old Is the Shepherd?

There are 25 sheep and 5 dogs in a flock. How old is the shepherd?

If possible, give this problem to your students before reading further, and then, with your own students' responses in mind, consider the questions in Reflect 2.1.

Reflect 2.1

What answer would you expect the students in our groups of third, sixth, and seventh graders to have given to the How Old Is the Shepherd problem?

What level of growth (as a percentage) would you expect to see in students' performance on this problem between third and sixth grade?

How much better would you expect seventh graders to perform on this problem than third graders or sixth graders?

Figure 2.1 shows a table of our results. The data detail an alarming lack of sense making. Middle-grades students demonstrated a success rate similar to that of third graders, although the distribution of approaches was different, with the third graders focusing on the operations that they knew. It is interesting to note that our data are even more discouraging than the results reported by Merseth (1993), who found that 3 out of 4 students answered this problem incorrectly.

	Added the numbers	Subtracted the numbers	Multiplied the numbers	Created a ratio	Other incorrect procedure	Suggested that no solution is possible
Third grade (n = 58)	76%	8%	0%	0%	14%	2%
Sixth grade (n = 71)	48%	9%	21%	8%	6%	8%
Seventh grade (n = 85)	48%	2%	17%	14%	9%	10%

Fig. 2.1. Third-, sixth- and seventh-grade students' responses to the How Old Is the Shepherd problem

Although our recent investigation offered empirical evidence that students were not focusing on the meaning of the problem to make decisions and model the situation mathematically, the weak performances of our middle-grades students suggested that they still did not understand that some problems cannot be solved or need to provide more information to be solvable. Figure 2.2 shows the work of one middle school student who detached the numbers in the problem from their contextual meanings and multiplied them to get a nonsensical result.

Students may be prompted to determine whether a problem provides enough information; however, when given a problem without this type of prompt, many students struggle to make sense of it. In general, the tendency of the middle-grades students in our study to apply an operation to a word problem mechanically and without thought revealed their lack of conceptual understanding and their years of exposure to tasks that simply required them to solve problems by adding, subtracting, multiplying or dividing the numbers given, instead of making sense of a situation.

Fig. 2.2. A middle-grades student's incorrect interpretation of the
How Old Is the Shepherd problem

What if you gave your young students several possible answers to discuss and choose among? Do you suppose that would lead them to think more carefully about the situation? Suppose that you presented them with a choice among, say—

- "The shepherd is 30 years old";

- "The shepherd is 20 years old"; and

- "It's not possible to tell the shepherd's age from the information that the problem gives."

Would your students be able to discern which of the three options would be the correct answer?

Try this with your students. Use an addition or subtraction problem that is aligned with your curriculum, and give your students choices of answers to talk about with their neighbors and accept or reject. Help them focus on making sense of the situation in context rather than the answers. Through the process of negotiating various options, students begin to understand the meanings of the operations in much deeper ways. If you approach this instruction with an emphasis on understanding the situation and the problem rather than on getting an answer, you will discover that the process of negotiating with children contributes to their learning. Furthermore, the process of ruling answers in or out will help them tackle multiple-choice tests with greater purpose.

Problem solving is more complex than extracting numbers from given problems. To grasp the context of a problem situation fully and interpret it accurately in different representations, as suggested in Essential Understanding 1e, students must make connections between the numbers and the meaning of the actions in the context. This thinking is quite different from applying a "key words" approach, which research suggests is not effective in helping students solve word problems (Griffin and Jitendra 2009). The key words approach does not support students in the process of sense making, especially when they face problems that have no key words, are expressed in language that is less than direct, contain unrelated information, or involve two or more steps. Karp, Bush, and Dougherty (2014) suggest that key words are part of a set of rules that "expire" because they quickly lose their usefulness and are not helpful when students approach more complex problems. Referring to the key words approach, Parmar, Cawley, and Frazita (1996) state that "the outcome of such training is that the student reacts to the cue word at a surface level of analysis and fails to perform a deep-structure analysis of the interrelationships among the word and the context in which it is embedded" (p. 427). Students need to analyze the full problem, taking every word and the contextual information into consideration, to build their understanding of the problem's meaning.

Working with Context in Word Problems

Context is essential to the development of understanding. As Fosnot and Dolk (2001) suggest, it should be used from the start as a means of "construction," rather than as a culminating or extending activity for "application" at the end of a unit of study. By presenting a situation and leaving students to chart their own path to a solution, you give them an opportunity to construct the mathematical ideas rather than simply apply an algorithm. If the context is "real," they will discuss and make sense of the situation, not just describe the steps in a procedure. This moves the focus from rules and procedures to conceptual problem solving. Reflect 2.2 probes ways to initiate this instructional emphasis in kindergarten.

Reflect 2.2

How do you think you might start using a context for learning addition and subtraction with kindergartners?

What types of word problems are commonly presented in a kindergarten mathematics lesson?

How might visuals support students in linking a problem set in a context with a solution?

Contextual situations should not be avoided just because students have not yet begun to read. Instead, they should become the starting place for developing operational understanding. Young children are in fact very strong problem solvers when presented with a story situation rather than just numbers (National Research Council 2001). For example, you might make a train, with passenger cars drawn on sheets of paper and counters serving as passengers (see fig. 2.3); you might even glue small photos of the students on ice-cream sticks to use as passengers. As a precursor to later work with written story problems, you can then tell your students stories about passengers getting on or off the train.

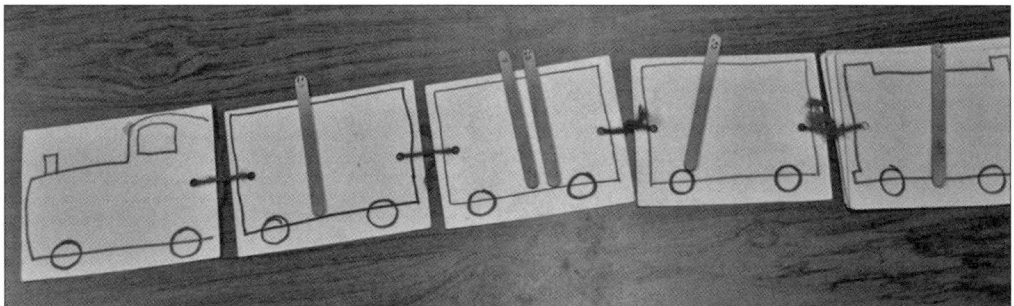

Fig. 2.3. A train with paper cars and 5 ice-cream sticks as people

Consider the following teacher-student dialogue, which shows how you might engage your students and develop their understanding and problem solving in the train context:

Teacher: Let's put 5 people on the train.

Raif: I put the 5 people on the train. But I didn't put anyone in the first car because it's the engine, and they are riders [*fig. 2.3 shows Raif's work*].

Teacher: At the first stop, 2 people get off the train. Can you show me what happens? [*Waits while Raif removes 2 people.*] Now how many people are on the train?

Raif: 3.

Teacher: At the next stop, 4 people get on the train. Show me what happens. [*Waits again while Raif adds 4 people.*] Now how many people are on the train?

Raif: I think 7.

Teacher: Let me show you how we would write what happened at that last train stop [*writes on the board*]: 3 + 4 = 7.

Teacher: [*Takes all the people off the train.*] Now, Raif, see if you can make up a problem that Lincoln can solve.

Raif: Put 2 people on the train.

Lincoln: [*Places 2 people on the train; see fig. 2.4.*] I put them in the same car.

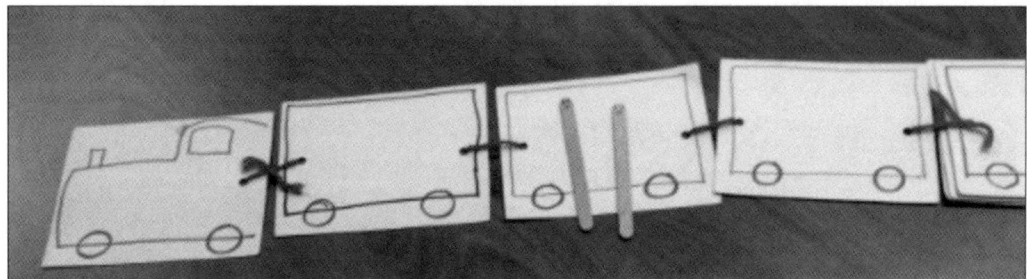

Fig. 2.4. Lincoln's train with 2 people

Raif: At the first stop, 6 people get on. How many people are on the train?

Lincoln: 8.

Teacher: Raif, can you and Lincoln tell what happened at the train stop in a number sentence?

[*Raif and Lincoln talk quietly to each other for a minute.*]

Lincoln: We think it is 2 + 6 = 8.

As students create these stories for one another, they begin to learn what mathematical language can be used that will make their partner add more people on the train and what they must say to induce him or her to take some people off the train. This is the beginning of the development of skill with word problems as the children expand their understanding of the meaning of the operations of addition and subtraction. This approach moves away from the use of key words to a central focus on comprehending the problem through the use of a process of storytelling and story interpreting.

When students begin this practice of sense making through work with stories, you can ask them a number of questions to help you gather information from them to be sure of their understanding:

- "What is happening in the story? Can you tell me in your own words?"
- "How many do you have?"
- "What do you need to think about?"

- "What will your answer be?" [*The number of cats, for example*]

- "Do you think your answer will be between _____ and _____?" [*A range, such as between 10 and 15, between 20 and 30, and so on*]

- "Can you act out this situation?"

- "What will the answer mean? How will you describe [*or label*] the answer?"

- "Can you find the parts of your problem in the number sentence you created?"

Remember, at first the focus should be on understanding the situation rather than on getting an answer.

Sorting Problems by Type

When your students are beginning to link problems with number sentences and to see patterns in word problems that lead to combining, separating, or comparing, they can benefit from sorting problems by type. Again, note that the focus here is not on the answer but on understanding the problem and its connections to mathematics. "Model with mathematics" is practice 4 in the Standards for Mathematical Practice (Common Core State Standards for Mathematics (CCSSM); National Governors Association Center for Best Practices and Council of Chief State School Officers [NGA Center and CCSSO] 2010, p. 7). The ability to model with mathematics is important to develop even with young learners. Students should be able to select a matching number sentence for a word problem. For example, offer your students the following problem.

Task: Kendra's Stuffed Animals

Kendra has 7 stuffed animals. Asha has 14 stuffed animals. How many more stuffed animals does Kendra need so that she will have as many stuffed animals as Asha?

Give students a choice among different number sentences, and ask them which one they think represents the situation:

$$14 - 7 = \square$$

$$7 + \square = 14$$

$$7 + 14 = \square$$

Use the questions in Reflect 2.3 to guide your thinking about how your students would be likely to respond.

Reflect 2.3

Consider the three equations 14 − 7 = □, 7 + □ = 14, and 7 + 14 = □.

Which equation (or equations) do you think your students would be likely to choose as the one that aligns with Kendra's Stuffed Animals?

Which equation is correct, even though students might miss it at first, because it is not a number sentence that they would usually think of for solving a problem of this type?

Figures 2.5–2.8 show the work of four second-grade students who sorted a variety of problems in an open-ended situation, grouping together problems that they thought were alike and explaining why they thought so. We were looking to see whether the students took note of the structures of the problems or whether the contexts were more important to them. This activity provided insights into students' approaches and thinking about solving word problems. Inspect the students' groupings and their reasoning, and then respond to the questions in Reflect 2.4.

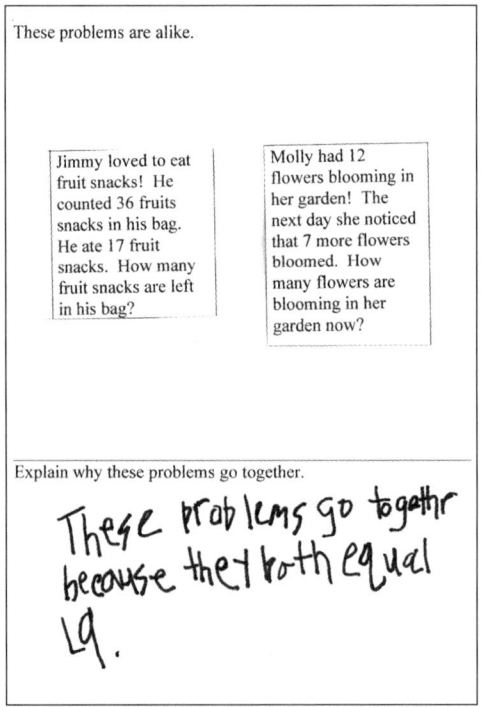

Fig. 2.5. Luke's grouping of word problems
as alike

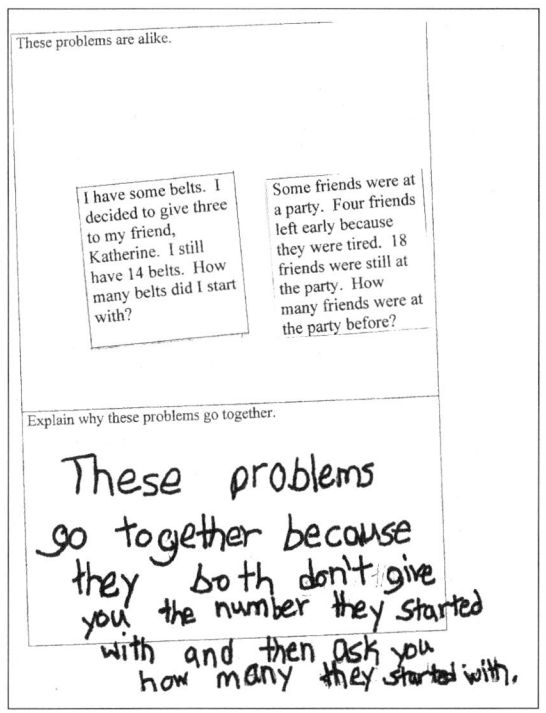

These problems are alike.

I have some belts. I decided to give three to my friend, Katherine. I still have 14 belts. How many belts did I start with?

Some friends were at a party. Four friends left early because they were tired. 18 friends were still at the party. How many friends were at the party before?

Explain why these problems go together.

These problems go together because they both don't give you the number they started with and then ask you how many they started with.

Fig. 2.6. Kendra's grouping of word problems as alike

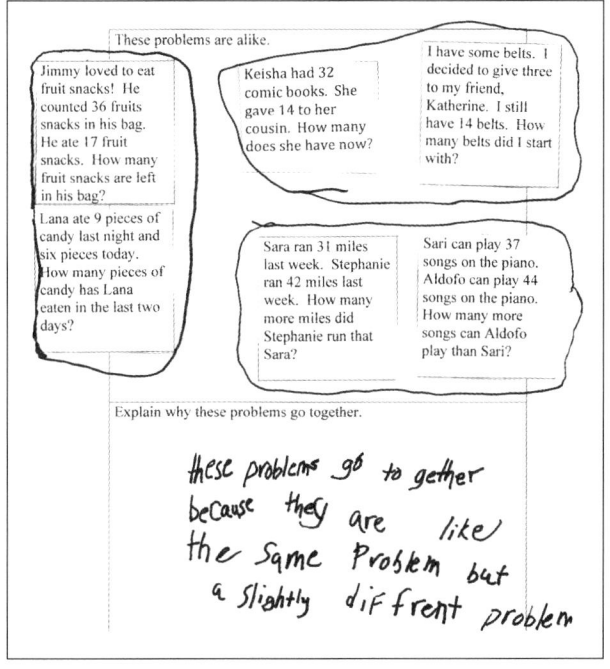

These problems are alike.

Jimmy loved to eat fruit snacks! He counted 36 fruits snacks in his bag. He ate 17 fruit snacks. How many fruit snacks are left in his bag?

Keisha had 32 comic books. She gave 14 to her cousin. How many does she have now?

I have some belts. I decided to give three to my friend, Katherine. I still have 14 belts. How many belts did I start with?

Lana ate 9 pieces of candy last night and six pieces today. How many pieces of candy has Lana eaten in the last two days?

Sara ran 31 miles last week. Stephanie ran 42 miles last week. How many more miles did Stephanie run that Sara?

Sari can play 37 songs on the piano. Aldofo can play 44 songs on the piano. How many more songs can Aldofo play than Sari?

Explain why these problems go together.

these problems go together because they are like the same problem but a slightly diffrent problem

Fig. 2.7. Sasha's grouping of word problems as alike

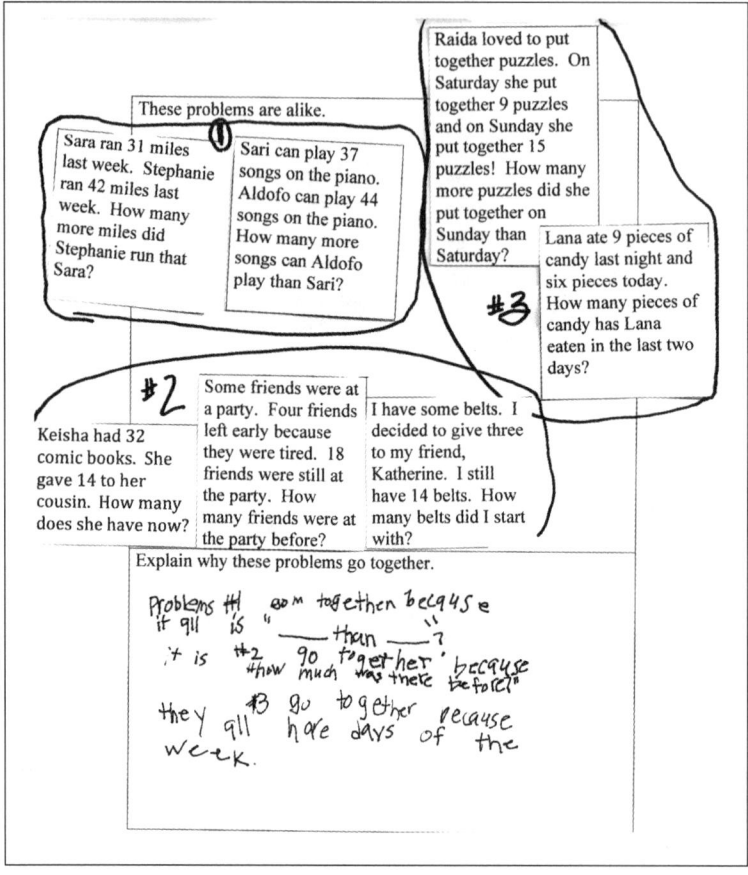

Fig. 2.8. Caroline's grouping of word problems as alike

Reflect 2.4

What reasoning do you think each student used in grouping the problems that he or she selected as alike?

Which students were paying attention to the underlying structures, and which were not?

What do these samples of students' groupings reveal that could inform the next instructional steps with each of these children?

It is useful to look closely at the work samples and note how these students generalized the rule that they used for grouping the problems as alike. Notice that Luke, whose work appears in fig. 2.5, did not use the structures of the problems that he grouped together to make connections. Rather, in making his pairing, he used the fact that the two problems have a common solution: 19. Luke decided that these problems go together simply because the "answer" is the same. Structure apparently was not important in the decision because Luke didn't notice that one is an addition problem and the other is a subtraction problem.

Using this type of sorting task can help you identify students whose thinking is similar to Luke's. Understanding how these students are thinking allows you to provide more opportunities for them to compare and contrast new problems with problems that they have solved before, strengthening their ability to make important connections among the structures of word problems.

Kendra's grouping of "like" problems (fig. 2.6) reveals more complex thinking. She noticed that both of the problems that she selected do not give the starting number ("start unknown" problem type). She observed that although the content of the problems is different, the structure is the same in both. Kendra's understanding appears to be sophisticated and capable of supporting her work with new problems. It seems likely that Kendra would associate new problems with problems that she had solved before.

Sasha's grouping of problems as alike (fig. 2.7) may reveal that she saw patterns in the types of problem and could sort them by type, though she struggled to name her groupings. Or her work may suggest that she used the contexts of the problems to group them. We asked Sasha to explain more about why she put certain problems together, and her reply was "because you do the same thing, like add or minus," but this is true of only one of Sasha's pairs. Her work thus demonstrates inconsistent or even immature thinking. Students may start with an idea that demonstrates tentative understanding of patterns in word problems, but they may not be able to continue the pattern. They may then begin to look for other ways to connect the problems by searching for similar contexts or similarities in how the problem begins or ends. Sasha's understanding was still developing: she knew that particular problems go together, and she could even solve them, but she struggled to name or identify the type of problem. Sasha would need more opportunities to talk about how she would solve a problem before actually solving it, as well as opportunities to explain her thinking process after she solved.

Caroline's sorting (fig. 2.8) reveals some focus on "key words" as a strategy for solving, suggesting that she had had some instruction on this approach. When we probed her sorting and grouping of the problems further, she said, "I am supposed to look for 'in all' to plus, and I can't find it." Caroline then resorted to other words in a problem to help her solve it and settled on the context, such as days of the week, to make sense of it. This is a common misconception for beginning students, who need many opportunities to discuss why and how certain words help or hinder their efforts to solve a problem. Sorting more word problems and discussing why and how other students grouped problems as alike and hearing their strategies might help Caroline understand the structures of the problems.

The work of each of these students represents a different level of development in solving word problems. Each sample suggests different possible next steps for instruction. Students must recognize the correspondence between symbols and problem elements and understand how symbols represent each element of a problem situation—that is, how mathematics models the situation. Children tend to select the format that maps directly to the way the problem is written and the way that they read the words. Instead of organizing their thinking around the order of the wording, instruction needs to focus their attention on the structure of the situation and the meaning of the scenario. Then students will begin to base their decisions about how problems should be grouped together on meaning and sense making.

Creating Problems to Deepen Understanding

Once your students are accustomed to discussing problems and linking mathematical situations with number sentences, you may want to reverse the process and have them create the problem situations. "What's the problem?" is a useful question to ask.

Initially, as a problem starter, you may want to give your students a story situation from a children's book that you are reading aloud to the whole class. Or you might give them a set of pictures or photos, a video clip, or everyday items (English 1998). Whether you are using a scenario from a video, a field trip, or a work of children's literature, start by asking your students what mathematical questions they might pose about the situation. Next, have the students create problems rooted in the context. By creating problems, the children will not only have ownership of the work but also develop a better understanding of the situations and of the operations that their problems call for, instead of merely operating on any numbers in the problem. This approach is also aligned with anchored instruction, which uses real-world situations or shared situations found in children's literature as the contexts for problems (Cognition and Technology Group at Vanderbilt 1990; Shih, Speer, and Babbitt 2011).

Another option is to anchor the instruction in a set of data, such as those shown in figure 2.9. Give one or more of these or similar sets of data to your students, and have them create problems. They can start by writing questions that they might want answered, and then they can move to creating word problems and matching equations.

Mariya had _____ stickers.

She found _____.

She lost _____.

Zac had 34 cookies.

Alix ate 14, and Janel ate 9 cookies.

Matt had 24 baseball cards and 25 football cards.

His brother had 12 cards.

Carly poured herself a bowl of Lucky Letters cereal.

She counted 57 consonants and 22 vowels in her bowl.

After eating some cereal, she counted only 35 letters.

Kelsie spent the day at the beach.

She saw 12 children swimming in the ocean.

15 children were playing in the sand.

20 children were splashing in the wading pool.

Fig. 2.9. Data sets for students to use in creating problems

Figure 2.10 shows some sample problems that second-grade students created from some of these data sets. This task aligns with an open-ended instructional approach: instead of solving a given problem, children work to create a problem of their own. By offering students multiple opportunities for thinking about different problems that would fit given situations, this approach ensures that *all* students have access to the task. As your students work through these or similar scenarios, be sure to encourage them to create a mixture of both addition and subtraction stories.

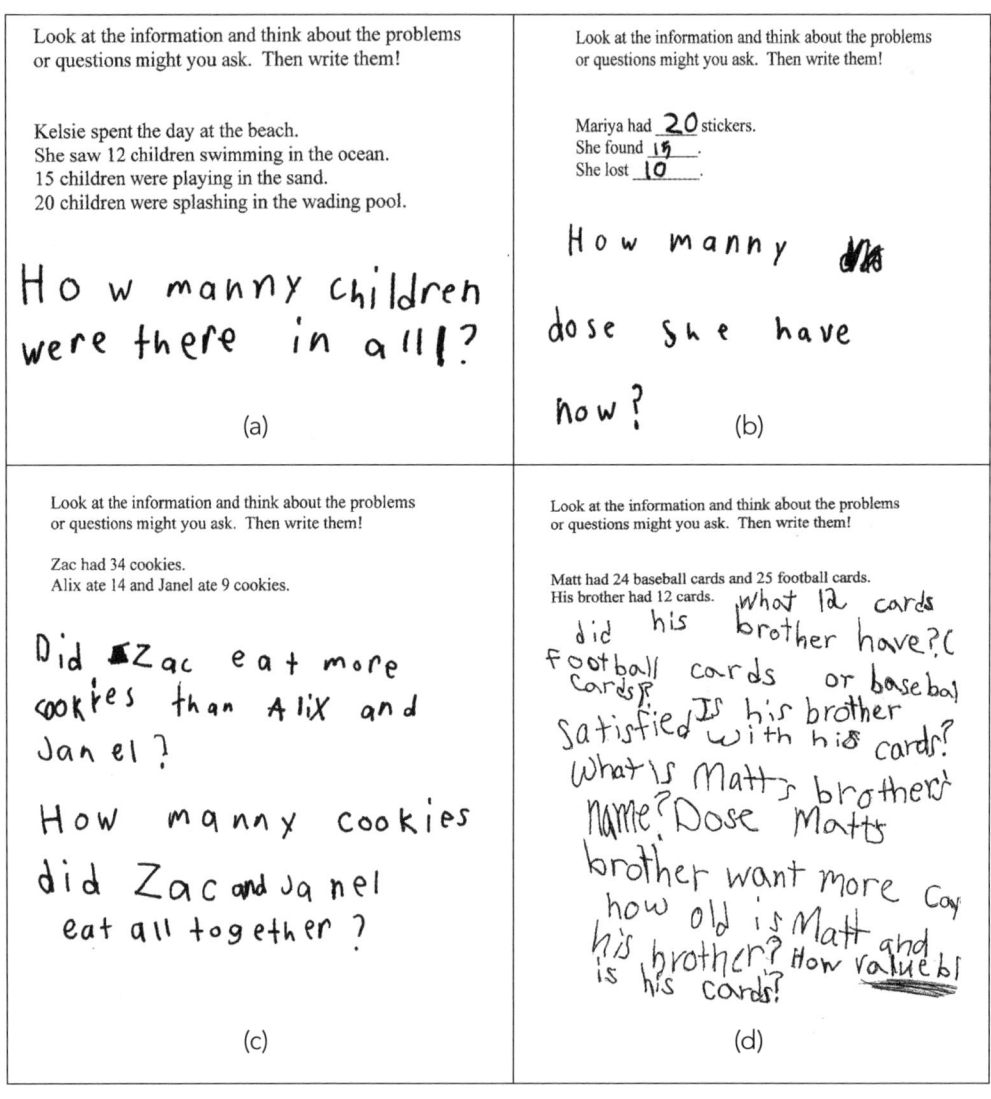

Fig. 2.10. Second graders create problems that align with information

Using the Structures of Additive Problems

Students who are taught to approach problems by looking at their structures through the use of a visual model are more likely to perform better than students who do not (Xin, Jitendra, and Deatline-Buchman 2005). They perform better immediately, over time, and in transferring the new learning to new tasks—and this is particularly true of students with disabilities. This approach helps students make sense of the problem as they connect the words in it with the diagram and the solution.

One way that you can approach this work of focusing students' attention on the structures of additive problems is through a template or graphic organizer. Children can work with the graphic organizer shown in figure 2.11 to think about additive situations.

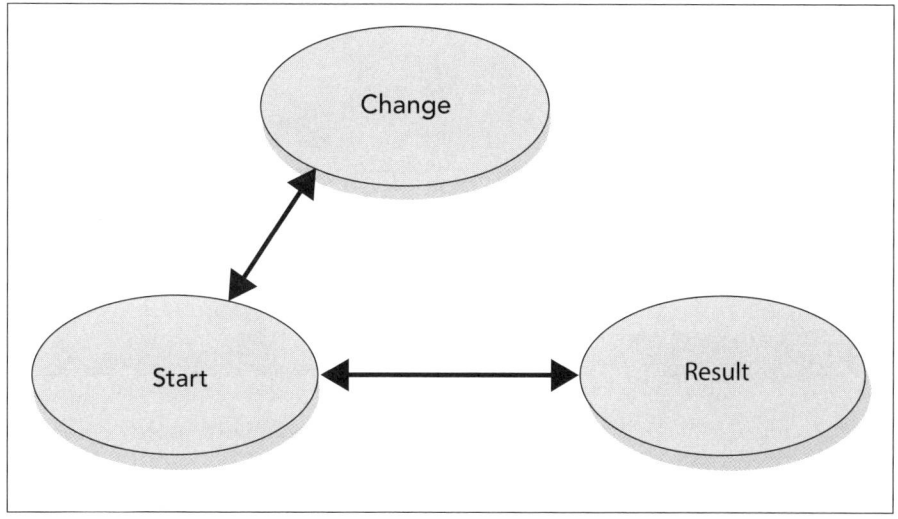

Fig. 2.11. A graphic organizer to support students' thinking about additive situations

To prepare this visual model for classroom use, open a clean manila folder, spread it flat, and use colored marking pens to draw your template or graphic organizer for teaching the structure of additive problems. Children can take a series of word problems and act them out by placing values (one, for "separate" problems; two, for "join" problems) on the organizing diagram to help them visualize the problem and the quantities to find the third amount (see fig. 2.12). Note that students start with "result unknown" problems in kindergarten and gradually move to problems of all types and subtypes ("add to," "take from," and "both addends unknown" situations) by the end of grade 2, when they are expected to "know from memory all sums of two one-digit numbers" (CCSSM 2.OA.2 [NGA Center and CCSSO 2010, p. 19]).

Figure 2.13 shows part of a table that appears in CCSSM (NGA Center and CCSSO 2010, p. 88) and highlights a variety of additive problems that represent all the structures. You can put these sample problems on cards and distribute them to your students to have them solve a variety of problems, or you can differentiate the problems for a variety of learners. The easiest problems to solve are of the types "result unknown," "total unknown," and "both addends unknown." The next level of difficulty consists of "change unknown" problems. "Start unknown problems" present the greatest challenge.

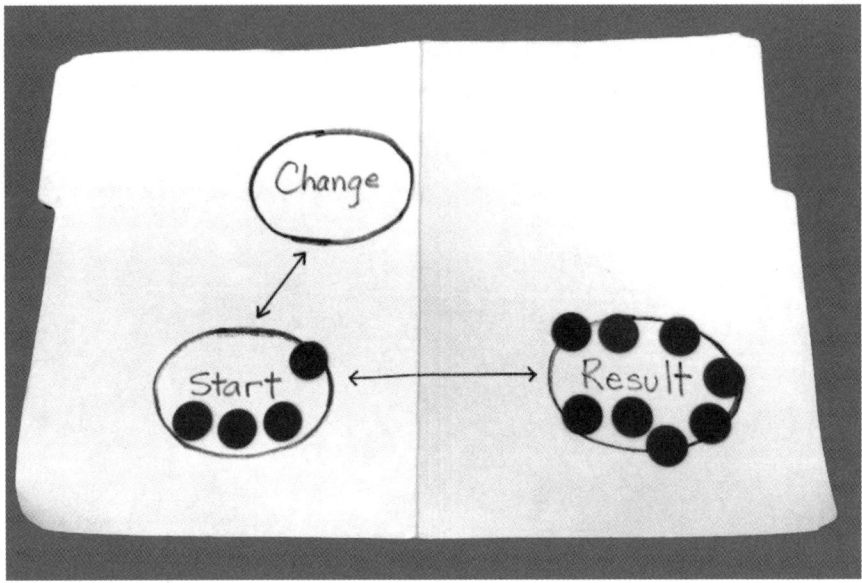

Fig. 2.12. A sample file folder for exploring the structure of additive problems by using the graphic organizer shown in figure 2.11

	Result Unknown	Change Unknown	Start Unknown
Add to	Two bunnies sat on the grass. Three more bunnies hopped there. How many bunnies are on the grass now? 2 + 3 = ?	Two bunnies were sitting on the grass. Some more bunnies hopped there. Then there were five bunnies. How many bunnies hopped over to the first two? 2 + ? = 5	Some bunnies were sitting on the grass. Three more bunnies hopped there. Then there were five bunnies. How many bunnies were on the grass before? ? + 3 = 5
Take from	Five apples were on the table. I ate two apples. How many apples are on the table now? 5 − 2 = ?	Five apples were on the table. I ate some apples. Then there were three apples. How many apples did I eat? 5 − ? = 3	Some apples were on the table. I ate two apples. Then there were three apples. How many apples were on the table before? ? − 2 = 3

	Total Unknown	Addend Unknown	Both Addends Unknown[1]
Put Together/ Take Apart[2]	Three red apples and two green apples are on the table. How many apples are on the table? 3 + 2 = ?	Five apples are on the table. Three are red and the rest are green. How many apples are green? 3 + ? = 5, 5 − 3 = ?	Grandma has five flowers. How many can she put in her red vase and how many in her blue vase? 5 = 0 + 5, 5 = 5 + 0 5 = 1 + 4, 5 = 4 + 1 5 = 2 + 3, 5 = 3 + 2

Fig. 2.13. Addition and subtraction problems representing different types and subtypes. Reprinted from CCSSM, table 1, "Common addition and subtraction situations" (NGA Center and CCSSO 2010, p. 88).

As children solve one- and eventually two-step word problems in situations involving adding to, taking from, putting together, taking apart, and comparing, with unknowns in all positions, they can cement the meanings of the problems by representing them with manipulative materials, drawings, and equations with a symbol for the unknown number. This work will lead students to understand a variety of equation formats in grade 1, as set out in CCSSM (see fig. 2.14).

Common Core State Standards for Mathematics, Grade 1

Work with addition and subtraction equations.

7. Understand the meaning of the equal sign, and determine if equations involving addition and subtraction are true or false. *For example, which of the following equations are true and which are false?* $6 = 6, 7 = 8 - 1, 5 + 2 = 2 + 5, 4 + 1 = 5 + 2.$

8. Determine the unknown whole number in an addition or subtraction equation relating three whole numbers. *For example, determine the unknown number that makes the equation true in each of the equations* $8 + ? = 11, 5 = \square - 3, 6 + 6 = \square.$

Fig. 2.14. Operations and Algebraic Thinking, CCSSM 1.OA.7–8
(NGA Center and CCSSO, p. 15)

The ability to make sense of equations like $2 + 7 = 4 + 5$ relies on another understanding—comprehension of the relational meaning of the equal sign. Research shows that the equal sign presents a consistent problem, even for older students (RAND Mathematics Study Panel 2003). Students must understand symbolism very well, especially symbols involving equality and inequality (greater than and less than) to be successful in mathematics—particularly algebra. In fact, some consider the lack of a full understanding of the equal sign to be one of the biggest stumbling blocks for students in learning algebra (Carpenter, Franke, and Levi 2003). Students must grasp the idea that the equal sign does not mean "makes" or "gives the answer," nor does it signal "the answer comes next." Instead, they must understand that it indicates the existence of an equivalence relationship, and it translates best into the words "is the same as." Students need to be reminded of and exposed to the fact that the equal sign is a relational symbol—not an operations symbol $(+, -, \times, \div)$—and that it does not always appear after the operation symbols in an equation.

Therefore, part of helping students to understand the equal sign involves moving them to a *relational strategy* and away from an *operational strategy*, which prompts them to calculate immediately to get "the answer." To assist them in making this transition, give them opportunities to work on tasks such as the following:

Task: Make It True

What number would make this number sentence true?

$$13 + 9 = 8 + 10 + \square$$

Students working with an operational strategy will immediately work to find the "answer" on each side, giving them the following:

$$22 = 18 + \square$$

Instead of having your students calculate each expression and find the individual "answers," move them to a relational strategy, which will induce them to compare numbers on both sides of the equal sign without computing the sums. For the preceding task, you might encourage this work by guiding them through the following thought process:

> 13 is 3 more than 10, and 9 is 1 more than 8. So the left side of the equation has 4 more than the right side of the equation. The answer has to be 4 for the two sides to be equivalent.

This approach highlights the use of a strategy that will benefit students as they continue on the path of thinking algebraically. It also aligns with the work of Kieran (2004), who suggests two important emphases in instruction on problem solving:

1. A focus on relationships rather than on the calculation of a numerical answer

2. A focus on the inverse relationship of operations (doing and undoing) rather than on the operations themselves

Linking Contexts with Representations

Providing students with powerful representations that they can continue to use from year to year is an important way to support them in tackling the challenges that they face in solving word problems. One useful tool that provides a visualization of a problem situation is a *tape diagram*. As explained in the glossary in CCSSM, a tape diagram is "a drawing that looks like a segment of tape, used to illustrate number relationships. Also known as strip diagram, bar model, fraction strip, or length model" (NGA Center and CCSSO 2010, p. 87), a tape diagram helps students sort out the relationship between quantities in a problem and create an image to support their reasoning. Figure 2.15 shows a generic example.

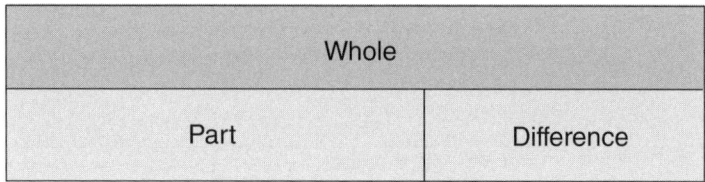

Fig. 2.15. An example of a generic tape diagram for a comparison problem

Before students choose a tape diagram as a tool to help them arrive at a solution, they need explicit support in understanding how they can use this representation to think about a word problem. This is true of the strategic use of any tool. Addition and subtraction situations are the place to begin, particularly by encouraging students to present the expression that models the situation horizontally rather than vertically and by starting with double ten frames. As students think about a situation, they can first use their counters in the ten frames to model the context. Consider Carter's Nickels.

Task: Carter's Nickels

Carter had 6 nickels. His mom gave him 7 more nickels. How many nickels did Carter have then?

You can encourage students to use a double ten frame mat to link to what might already be a familiar tool for modeling this problem ($6 + 7 = \square$) with the new tool. Figure 2.16 shows the problem on two ten frames. It is important to remember to use a familiar diagram to teach a new concept and to use a familiar concept to teach a new diagram. Attempting to combine both—a new concept and a new diagram—is not likely to be a successful way to help students make a smooth transition from what they know to what they don't know.

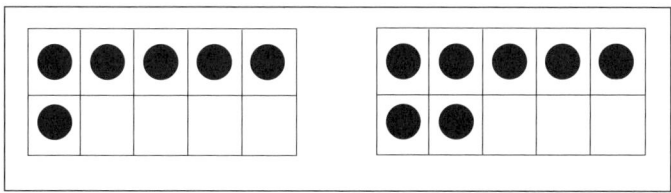

Fig. 2.16. Showing $6 + 7 = \square$ on two ten frames to solve Carter's Nickels

The next step is to move the students to a visual with "boxes" enclosing the counters in two groups—the nickels that Carter had at first and the nickels that his mother gave him. The boxes should have the same height but different lengths, determined by the number of nickels in each group, as in figure 2.17. The sum then represents the joining of the two groups. The students are now seeing how to model the problem with a tape diagram.

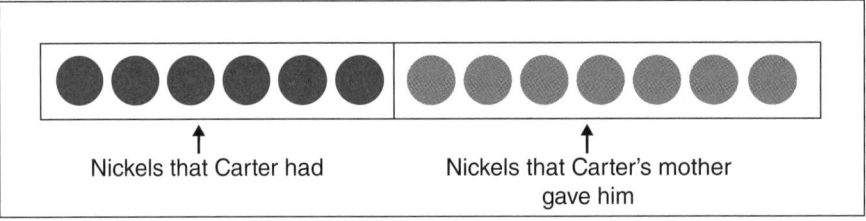

Fig. 2.17. Showing 6 + 7 = □ with a tape diagram

Students can also use a tape diagram to explore and model a subtraction problem of a different type. Consider Jorge's Cookies, a task that is set in a different context and offers students a greater challenge because it presents them with an "unknown" (or an empty space), as part of the whole:

> **Task: Jorge's Cookies**
>
> Jorge has 12 cookies. Some are chocolate chip, and some are peanut butter. If 7 of the cookies are chocolate chip, how many cookies are peanut butter?

To model Jorge's Cookies, students can work with a part-part-whole model that lets them see the two parts of the quantity by putting counters directly in the spots where they represent what is known, as in figure 2.18. Then the students must consider the whole as the full length of the model and solve for the missing part. This is not a simple next step.

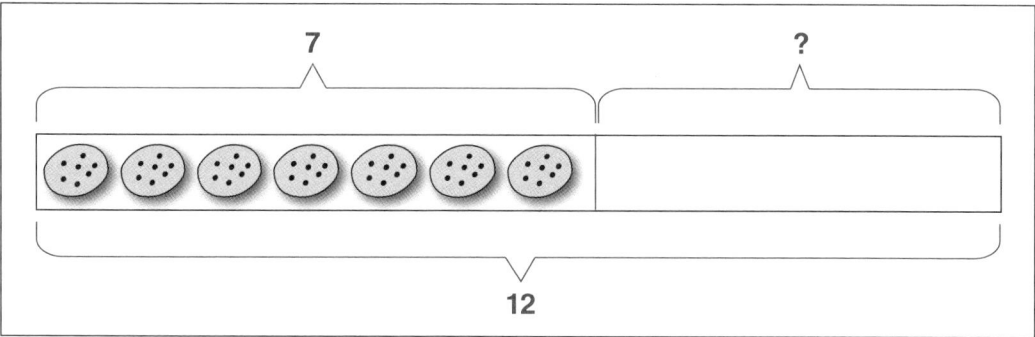

Fig. 2.18. Using cookie counters to explore Jorge's Cookies, a situation with an unknown part

To help the students progress in their learning, have them first place actual items in the strip, then sketch items in it, and finally write numbers in the strip. Guide students explicitly in thinking about the equation $12 = 7 + \square$. To find the unknown represented by $\square$, students need support in thinking about the empty box in the equation and how it relates to the empty box in the tape diagram. Computationally, they can solve the problem by using either subtraction ($12 - 7 = \square$) or addition ($12 = 7 + \square$), in the second case thinking, "What do I add to 7 to equal 12?" Figure 2.19 shows progressions in the use of tape diagrams to represent addition and subtraction.

The context that you provide and the questions that you ask are critical in such situations. Your questions should relate the components of the tape diagram to the parts, and the length of the tape to the whole, reinforcing the part-part-whole understanding that students are developing.

As Beckmann (2004) states, "With the aid of simple strip diagrams, children can use straightforward reasoning to solve many challenging story problems conceptually" (p. 46). But the visual representation can be useful to students only if they can link it explicitly to their comprehension of the problem and use the representation as a demonstration of their thinking. By encouraging your students to lay out the components in thoughtful ways, you can help them choose the correct operation on the basis of their understanding of the problem situation rather through a procedural approach that involves gathering any numbers in the problem and operating on them, as most students did in responding to the How Old Is the Shepherd problem, discussed at the beginning of this chapter.

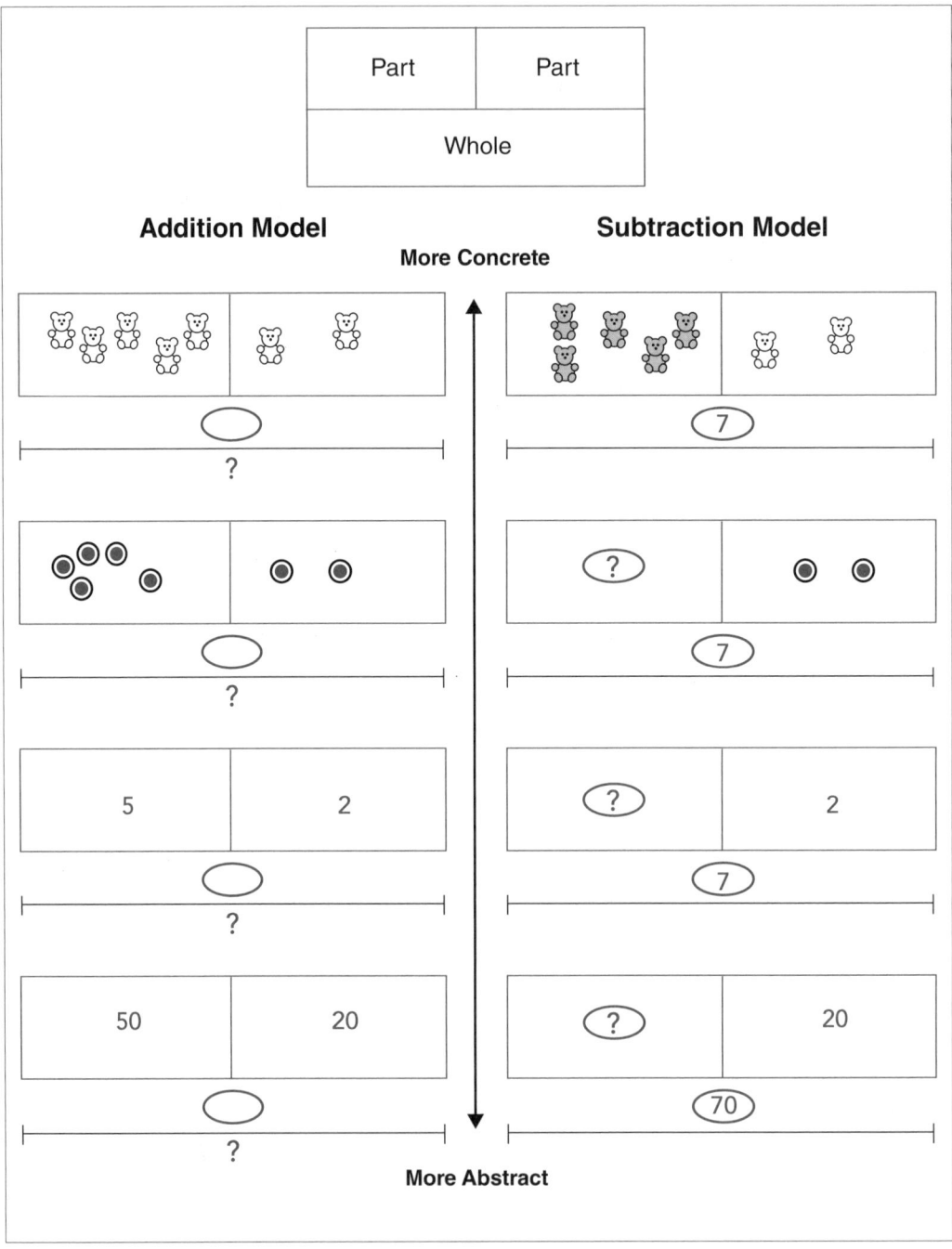

Fig. 2.19. Progressions in the use of tape diagrams for addition and subtraction

Interpreting Subtraction Problems

Some students mistakenly think of subtraction only as "take away." In fact, some of their parents or teachers may have mistakenly encouraged this idea by saying "take away" when they read an expression, substituting that phrase in place of the subtraction sign. For example they might read "13 – 5" as "thirteen take away five." Faced with contextual problems, these students then have trouble linking subtraction with scenarios that actually present a "compare" or "missing addend" situation (Kamii and Lewis 2003). This limited interpretation can complicate students' efforts to understand subtraction—efforts that Reflect 2.5 asks you to pause and consider.

Reflect 2.5

Do you think students find subtraction more challenging to understand and "do" than addition? Why or why not?

What types of word problems do you think you should pose to students to support their ability to make sense of subtraction?

What language do you think can support students' understanding of subtraction situations?

As stated in the Draft Progressions developed by the Common Core State Standards Writing Team (2011) on counting and cardinality in kindergarten and operations and algebraic thinking in K–grade 5, "Learning to think of and solve subtractions as unknown addend problems make subtraction as easy as addition (or even easier), and it emphasizes the relationship between addition and subtraction" (p. 15). Subtraction has a complexity that can be lessened for children by "thinking addition." In adding, they start with a number, and at first they may use their fingers or a manipulative to count on, say, 3 more: 8 + 3 = 11. In subtracting, they must know how far 8 is from 11 and mentally keep track of the counts as they count up (often with no materials). They must also know to stop counting when they reach the target number. This is not unlike the way in which many adults typically make change, "thinking addition" as they count up to the total, rather than subtracting in their heads. Birds at the Feeder is a task that invites students to "think addition."

Task: Birds at the Feeder

7 birds were at the feeder outside the classroom window. Some more birds flew to the feeder. Then 11 birds were at the feeder. How many more birds flew to the feeder?

Do a "think aloud" in which you and your students talk about how to approach this problem from a "think addition" perspective. You might say, "I see birds at the feeder. First, there are 7. Then I see birds 8, 9, 10, and 11 come to the feeder." Counting on in this way is far easier than counting back. When students attempt to solve subtraction problems that have a part-part-whole structure, they often find the "think addition" strategy helpful. This is especially true of students with disabilities (Peltenburg, van den Heuvel-Panhuizen, and Robitzsch 2012).

Using Language to Develop Context

When you use the "compare" model in subtraction situations, you may sometimes find that the language "how many more than" is challenging for your students and can be a barrier to their understanding. In a study of student's work with "compare" problems, Hudson (1983) found that when teachers used the language "How many will not get...?" or "Who won't get...?" in posing problems, their students were more successful as they tried to count and match items accurately to compare quantities. Consider the wording in the task Azita's Forks, for example.

> **Task: Azita's Forks**
>
> Azita has 4 forks to use to set the table for the dinner. The dinner will have 9 guests. How many more forks does Azita need so that each guest will have a fork? If Azita doesn't find more forks, how many guests won't get a fork?

"How many won't get?" provides an important bridge to "How many more are needed?" and helps students connect the words that they are likely to see in a word problem with a more meaningful way of thinking about comparisons.

"How many fewer?" also presents difficulties for students, who find this question more challenging than "How many more?" Try the following task, Lena's Cents, as well as Azita's Forks, with your students to determine which language they find more meaningful.

> **Task: Lena's Cents**
>
> Lena has 12 cents. Rocco has 18 cents. How many more cents does Lena need to have as many as Rocco?

You can link both these tasks visually with the part-part-whole model by focusing on the central subtraction idea, "When you are looking for the *difference*, you are subtracting." Figure 2.20 illustrates this idea in a tape diagram. Remind your students that the answer in a subtraction problem is called the *difference*. However, it is also important that students recognize that the difference represents the amount that could be added to the other part to create the whole. By emphasizing that every subtraction problem can be thought of as an addition problem, you will be emphasizing the inverse relationship between the two operations.

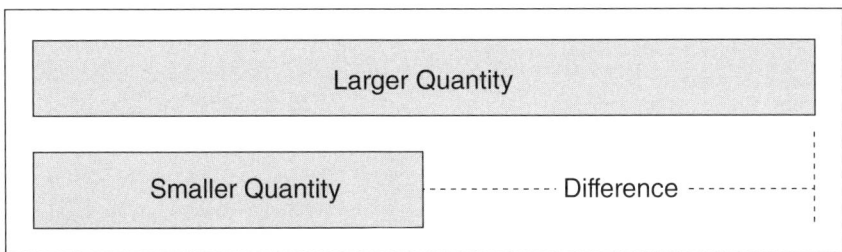

Fig. 2.20. A generic tape diagram for the "compare" model in subtraction (or addition)

By working with tape diagrams, students can begin to mentally sort quantities that are known from quantities that are unknown, in meaningful ways. In the relationships between these quantities, they can begin to see patterns that lead them to decide, "Do I add? Or do I subtract?" Using a tape diagram, they can represent the relationship among the quantities in Azita's Forks as shown in figure 2.21.

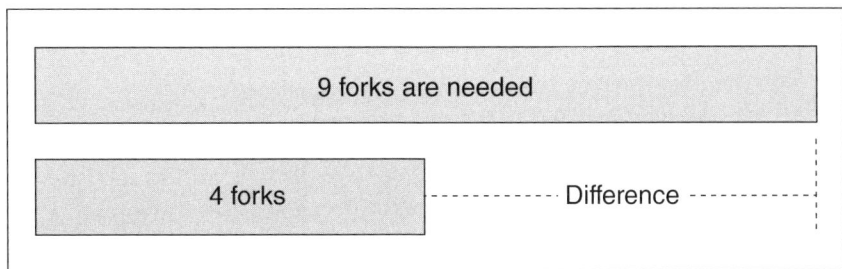

Fig. 2.21. A tape diagram for Azita's Forks, representing how many guests will not get a fork as the *difference*

Demonstrating Understanding with a Translation Task

One way to assess whether your students can use representations flexibly is to give them a translation task (Van de Walle et al. 2014). Figure 2.22 shows a translation task template (available in a larger, classroom-ready format in Appendix 3 at More4U). The template allows students to demonstrate their understanding of an addition or subtraction problem by—

- creating a word problem;
- making a visual model of the problem;
- representing the problem in an equation; and
- giving an explanation of their thinking.

Equation	Word problem
Model	Explanation

Fig. 2.22. Translation task template for students

Note that depending on the age of the students, you can adapt the headings to accommodate students who are—

- studying numbers rather than operations;
- can tell a story orally but cannot write it; or

- can represent a story by drawing but do not have other concrete materials available.

As children move among multiple representations, including an appropriate context in a story problem, the likelihood increases that they will form the concept correctly and integrate it into a collection of interrelated ideas.

Figures 2.23–2.26 show four second-grade students' work on a translation task, including one sample showing an unsuccessful word problem. Whether you give the translation task to the whole class or to small groups of students, their work can provide you with useful information for pinpointing their strengths and weaknesses. Once you have collected and assessed the data from the task, you can carefully target instruction to match students' needs.

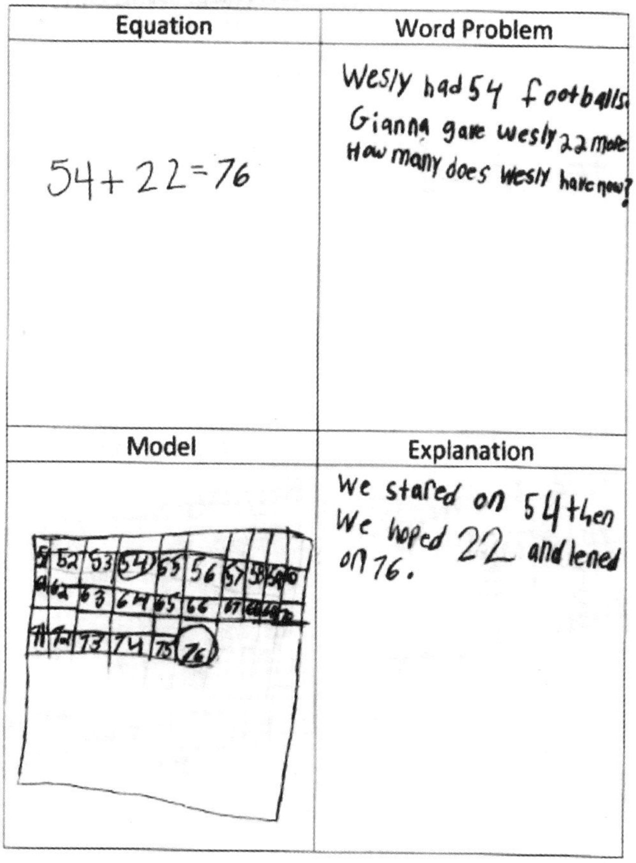

Equation	Word Problem
$54 + 22 = 76$	Wesly had 54 footballs. Gianna gave Wesly 22 more. How many does Wesly have now?
Model	**Explanation**
51 52 53 54 55 56 57 58 59 60 / 61 62 63 64 65 66 67 68 69 70 / 71 72 73 74 75 (76)	We stared on 54 then we hoped 22 and lened on 76.

Fig. 2.23. A student uses a portion of a hundreds chart to determine an answer to a story problem.

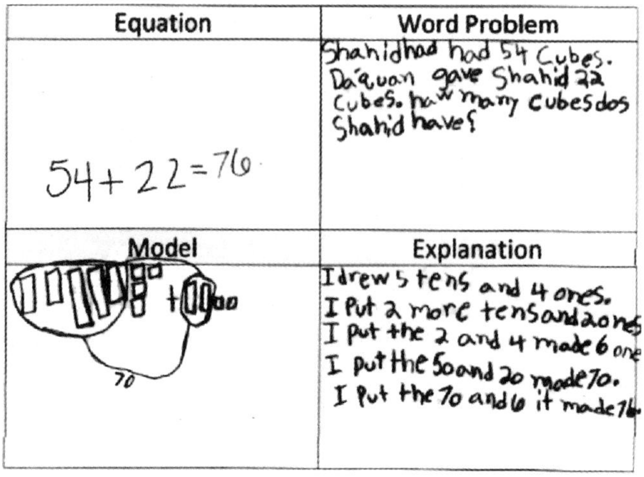

Equation	Word Problem
$54 + 22 = 76$	Shahid had had 54 Cubes. Daquan gave Shahid 22 Cubes. how many cubes dos Shahid have?
Model	**Explanation**
	I drew 5 tens and 4 ones. I put 2 more tens and 2 ones. I put the 2 and 4 made 6 one. I put the 50 and 20 made 70. I put the 70 and 6 it made 76.

Fig. 2.24. A student draws a representation of base-ten materials, with the explanation clarifying the process.

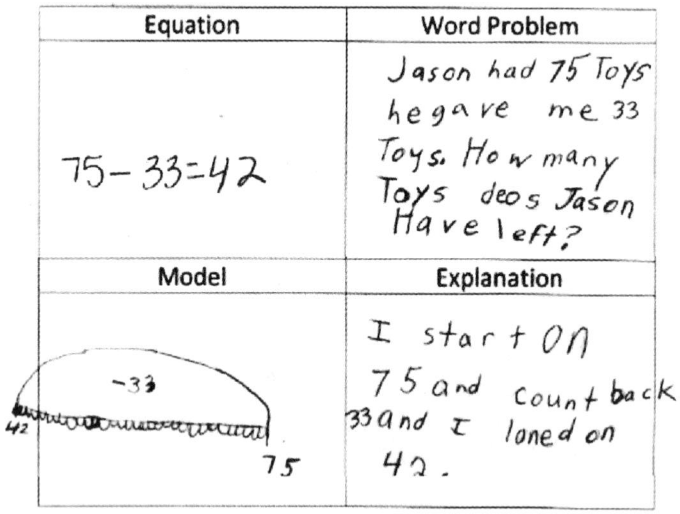

Equation	Word Problem
$75 - 33 = 42$	Jason had 75 Toys he gave me 33 Toys. How many Toys deos Jason Have left?
Model	**Explanation**
	I start on 75 and count back 33 and I loned on 42.

Fig. 2.25. A student uses a number line to represent a subtraction situation.

Equation	Word Problem
$54 + 22 = 76$	Danyle had 54 Hot dogs. jason gave me 22 more. how many Hot dogs do I have?

Model	Explanation
$54 + 22 = 76$ $(50+4) + (20+2)$ $50+20=70$ $4+2=6$ $70+6=\boxed{76}$	I broke apart 54 and it made 50+4 then I broke a part 22 it made 20+2 I added 50+20=70 and then I r_4 + 4+2=6 and I put 70+6=76.

Fig. 2.26. A student demonstrates the use of the "breaking apart" approach to decompose numbers and then add.

Summary: Learners, Curriculum, Instruction, and Assessment

Understanding addition and subtraction sets the stage for understanding all the other operations that students will encounter in years to come. Helping students develop this understanding requires a conscious look at the four components identified in the Introduction: learners, curriculum, instructional strategies, and assessment. Each component is clearly evident in this chapter's consideration of developing understanding of addition and subtraction by giving students many opportunities to encounter and work with these operations in "real" contexts. Learners need to be engaged in tasks that are set in a context to build reasoning and sense-making skills from the start. The curriculum should also provide a variety of problems in different contexts, especially avoiding reducing problems to single words or naked numbers to obtain a solution. In this regard, Fosnot and Dolk (2002, p. 28) underscore an important truth:

> When the context is a good one, the children talk about the situation. When a problem is camouflaged school mathematics, children talk about numbers abstractly; they lose sight of the problem as they try to figure out what the teacher wants.

You also highlight the use of problem-solving strategies when you foster multiple approaches and representations and discuss them with your students as integral parts of your instructional approach. This exploration of different ideas stimulates the thinking of children who didn't come up with these ideas on their own, allowing them to embrace or adopt new approaches for future use.

Finally, you must assess your students in informal ways, such as reviewing their work on the translation task, to gain access to their thinking so that you can answer the critical question, Did they actually get it? Or did they just think they did, but they—and you—will find out on the formal end-of-year assessment that large gaps remained in their full understanding.

Conclusion

This chapter is filled with samples of children's work that highlight the kinds of activities that are critical to moving students from a narrow focus on getting answers and learning algorithms quickly to an emphasis on the context and meaning of the operations as they relate to actual situations that children encounter. The chapter has discussed the importance of the knowledge and understanding that you bring to the work of creating and adapting problems in a context, starting even in kindergarten. By carefully structuring conversations around sense making rather than merely calling out answers and moving on, you bring to the forefront the value of understanding what the problem is asking. By using the samples of student work included in this chapter or by creating fictitious student work for your own class discussions, you will not only motivate your students to critique the reasoning of others but also shift the conversation from naked answers to mathematical reasoning about relationships between and among quantities.

into practice

Chapter 3
Strategies for Basic Facts for Addition and Subtraction

Big Idea 2
The mathematical foundations for understanding computational procedures for addition and subtraction of whole numbers are the properties of addition and place value.

Essential Understanding 2*a*
The commutative and associative properties for addition of whole numbers allow computations to be performed flexibly.

Essential Understanding 2*b*
Subtraction is not commutative or associative for whole numbers.

Why do students in the primary grades continually struggle in their attempts to learn and retain basic facts? Teachers often worry that students' lack of knowledge of basic facts is holding them back in their mathematical development. They observe students using ineffective and even laborious techniques to compute and remember their facts. They recognize that fact mastery can be a determinant of movement to higher-level mathematics, with students stumbling when they attempt to integrate weak computation skills with more sophisticated concepts.

An important component of basic fact knowledge is conceptual understanding of basic fact strategies. By presenting tasks that encourage student-developed or student-derived strategies for obtaining or establishing basic facts, you can help your students make sense of the facts, using what they know about number combinations and relationships among facts and connecting them through common strategies (Baroody 2006; Chapin and Johnson 2006). By developing their own strategies and having multiple opportunities to identify relationships among basic facts and

Common Core State Standards for Mathematics

Related to the Big Idea and Essential Understandings for Chapter 3

Grade 1 (1.OA.3–6, 8)

3. Apply properties of operations as strategies to add and subtract. *Examples: If 8 + 3 = 11 is known, then 3 + 8 = 11 is also known. (Commutative property of addition.) To add 2 + 6 + 4, the second two numbers can be added to make a ten, so 2 + 6 + 4 = 2 + 10 = 12. (Associative property of addition.)*

4. Understand subtraction as an unknown-addend problem. For example, subtract 10 – 8 by finding the number that makes 10 when added to 8.

5. Relate counting to addition and subtraction (e.g., by counting on 2 to add 2).

6. Add and subtract within 20, demonstrating fluency for addition and subtraction within 10. Use strategies such as counting on; making ten (e.g., 8 + 6 = 8 + 2 + 4 = 10 + 4 = 14); decomposing a number leading to a ten (e.g., 13 – 4 = 13 – 3 – 1 = 10 – 1 = 9); using the relationship between addition and subtraction (e.g., knowing that 8 + 4 = 12, one knows 12 – 8 = 4); and creating equivalent but easier or known sums (e.g., adding 6 + 7 by creating the known equivalent 6 + 6 + 1 = 12 + 1 = 13).

8. Determine the unknown whole number in an addition or subtraction equation relating three whole numbers. For example, determine the unknown number that makes the equation true in each of the equations 8 + ? = 11, 5 = □ – 3, 6 + 6 = □.

Grade 2 (2.OA.2)

2. Fluently add and subtract within 20 using mental strategies. By end of Grade 2, know from memory all sums of two one-digit numbers.

Grade 2 (2NB.5, 8, 9)

5. Fluently add and subtract within 100 using strategies based on place value properties of operations, and/or the relationship between addition and subtraction.

8. Mentally add 10 or 100 to a given number 100–900, and mentally subtract 10 or 100 from a given number 100–900.

9. Explain why addition and subtraction strategies work, using place value and the properties of operations.

(National Governors Association Center for Best Practices and Council of Chief State School Officers [NGA Center and CCSSO] 2010, pp. 15–19) number combinations, students progress naturally to computational fluency. You can then provide your students with tasks that build *procedural fluency*, which the National Research Council (2001) describes as skill in carrying out procedures "flexibly, accurately, efficiently, and appropriately" (p. 5).

Young students need to be encouraged to develop their understanding of addition and subtraction by using manipulative tools to represent the quantities and actions in a problem. These concrete representations are crucial to understanding the concepts of one-to-one correspondence and magnitude. Young students make a set, length, or other type of model for each value (depending on the context of the problem), and then they typically "count all" to find the total. As they progress to fluency, many children continue to use a "count all" strategy, with mixed results. After repeated use of this approach, some students do begin to commit the basic number facts to memory, but a substantial number continue to use "count all" or "take away" strategies, relying on their fingers, manipulatives, or pictures well into the upper elementary years and beyond.

Although "count all" is a perfectly reasonable beginning strategy, it can impede students' ultimate development of fluency. We have observed students counting on their fingers, bobbing their heads to keep track as they count, or even drawing a series of hash marks as they find addition facts that they have seen many times before or sums that are greater than are practical to obtain with that strategy. While these students are often successful in determining correct answers, their efficiency, speed, and accuracy may be reduced. The Common Core State Standards for Mathematics (CCSSM; NGA Center for Best Practices and Council of Chief State School Officers [NGA Center and CCSSO] 2010) expect students in grade 2 to add and subtract numbers fluently up to 20; thus, students need to have a variety of strategies to bridge from "count all" and "take away" techniques to more fluent mental math strategies. By encouraging the use of student-led or student-derived work with strategies and the explicit teaching of these strategies, you can help your students develop more efficient approaches for retrieving and retaining basic addition and subtraction facts.

You can facilitate the development of student-derived fact strategies, common addition and subtraction fact strategies, and computational fluency by posing a series of tasks that encourage your students to make important connections. This chapter explores three types of tasks, identified below by what they engage students in doing:

1. Deriving their own strategies

2. Analyzing another student's strategy or strategies

3. Developing fluency through an activity called "Spin, Circle, and Solve" and other activities or games.

Working with Student-Developed Strategies

After your students have had prior experiences in representing whole number values with cubes and lengths and have drawn pictures to match addition situations in word problems set in a variety of contexts, you can give them a task such as the following to facilitate their understanding of patterns and relationships among addition facts. This task engages them in working with basic fact cards—typically, cards that show an addition problem and ask for the sum to complete the addition fact.

Task: Sorting Basic Facts

Sort the basic fact cards in a way that makes sense to you. Group facts that you think belong together, and then explain your thinking.

In this task, students sort through basic fact cards and identify facts that they can put together by a rule of their own choosing. Figure 3.1 shows a graphic organizer for the task (available in a larger format in Appendix 3 at More4U).

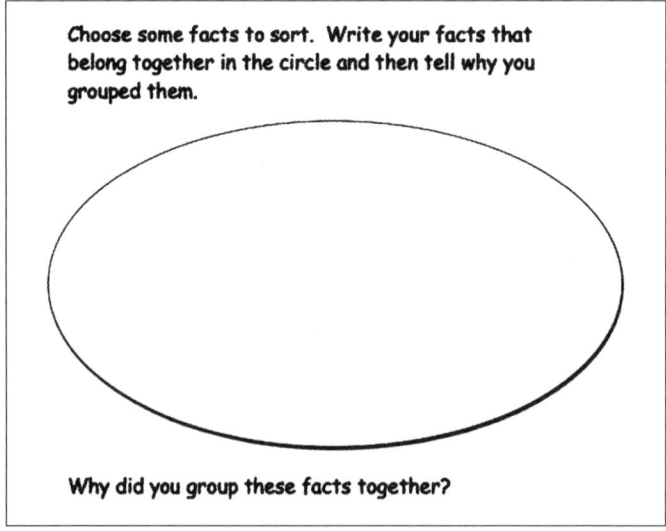

Fig. 3.1. Graphic organizer for the Sorting Basic Facts task

Students' misconceptions can come to light in this task, sometimes revealed in their reliance on superficial sorting techniques. For example, a student might group expressions that have an addend in common, such as 4 + 1 and 4 + 5, choosing them because both have a 4. Or some students might put expressions together because of the way that written number symbols look to them. For instance, we have seen students group fact cards that they say show "straight" numbers. One student explained "straight" numbers as numbers like 4, 7, and 1, and "round" numbers as numbers like 3, 6, and 9. Clearly, this student was thinking about how she formed the numerals when writing them. When she was learning to write numbers, someone may even have told her that certain numbers are "straight" and others are "round."

However, by having opportunities to hear other students' thinking and by focusing on representations, explanations, and models, students gradually begin to distinguish, use, and describe more sophisticated relationships. When students demonstrate their reasoning and explain why they have connected particular facts, they become more mindful of different—and sometimes unusual—relationships between and among addition facts.

Once your students have performed the sorting task with many different fact cards, you can think about how you want to teach the strategies in a more explicit way, using what the students have told you about their own thinking and connecting it with their own strategies. Without knowing your students' misconceptions and perceptions, you are likely to miss valuable opportunities to dispel a misunderstanding or to reveal an interesting or useful strategy. When you give students opportunities to sort fact cards and identify their own strategies for obtaining the facts *before* you teach specific common strategies, you can often make connections among facts explicitly and show relationships that you know will make sense to them. This process can enhance and strengthen your students' development of fluency.

Reflect 3.1 explores one student's grouping of addition facts on the Sorting Basic Facts task. Use the questions to guide your consideration of this grouping before examining the student's work, shown in figure 3.2.

Reflect 3.1

In the Sorting Basic Facts task, one student grouped the following facts:

$$9 + 1 = 10 \qquad 2 + 8 = 10 \qquad 7 + 3 = 10$$

If you had chosen to group these facts, what "rule" would you have used?

Does your rule for the grouping align with the reasoning that the student shared in her work, shown in figure 3.2?

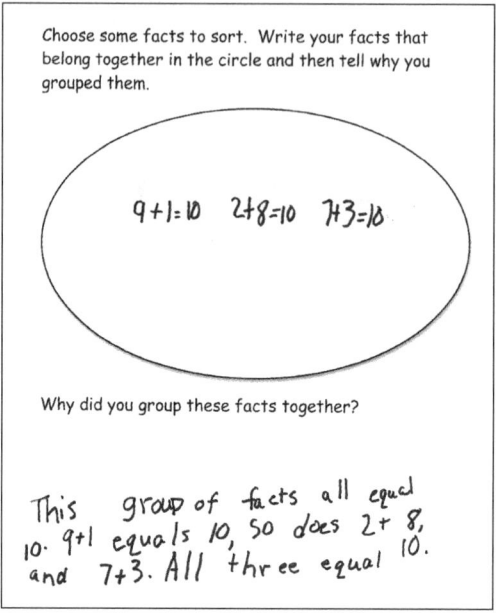

Fig. 3.2. A student's grouping of addition facts and explanation for her sorting

This student grouped facts that are sums of 10. By beginning to associate all the pairs of numbers that sum to 10, she demonstrated that she was beginning to understand that 10 is an important benchmark sum. You could ask such a student to show her idea or justify it by using a ten frame, cubes, or Cuisenaire rods (as "trains"). Any of these models could also help her and other students make connections from concrete or semi-concrete models to more abstract number sentences.

This sorting and grouping process can give students a purpose and direction as they approach strategies in a more explicit way. Students can analyze one another's sorting decisions and rationales and then discuss how the facts are similar. If you were working with a student who grouped number facts for sums of 10, you could build on this grouping to introduce the "make 10" strategy naturally and effectively. By sorting, describing, and eventually naming the strategy, students develop mental connections among the facts, and they call on the strategy to help them retrieve the facts and retain them in long-term memory.

Reflect 3.2 focuses on a different sorting and probes possible reasons why this student put these facts together. Respond to the questions before turning to the student's work, shown in figure 3.3.

Reflect 3.2

A student grouped together the following expressions in the Sorting Basic Facts task:

$$5 + 6 \qquad 7 + 6 \qquad 5 + 8 \qquad 9 + 6$$

What reasoning might a student use to sort these combinations of addends and group them together?

Compare your ideas about possible reasoning with the explanation provided by the student, whose work appears in figure 3.3.

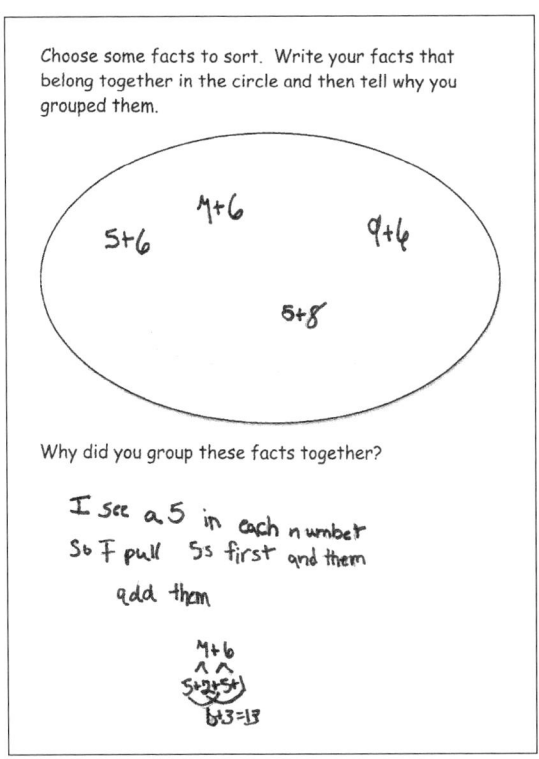

Fig. 3.3. A student's grouping of addition expressions and explanation for his sorting

The student said that he was "seeing" a 5 in each number. In expressing himself in this way, he appears to have visualized the 5 as though the value were represented as a row in a ten frame. He decomposed each number and added the 5s first and then the "extras." Although this strategy is certainly not a standard or popular one for addition, it made sense to the student, for whom it might even have been a precursor to successful use of the "make 10" strategy.

Reflect 3.3 focuses on another unusual strategy and grouping. Consider the possible reasoning behind this student's grouping before turning to figure 3.4, which shows her work and reasoning.

Reflect 3.3

A student's grouping of the following addend combinations reflects an unexpected strategy:

4 + 8   6 + 4   8 + 6

What strategy might this student have used to group these expressions together?

Compare your prediction of the student's strategy with the explanation that she gave for her grouping, shown in figure 3.4.

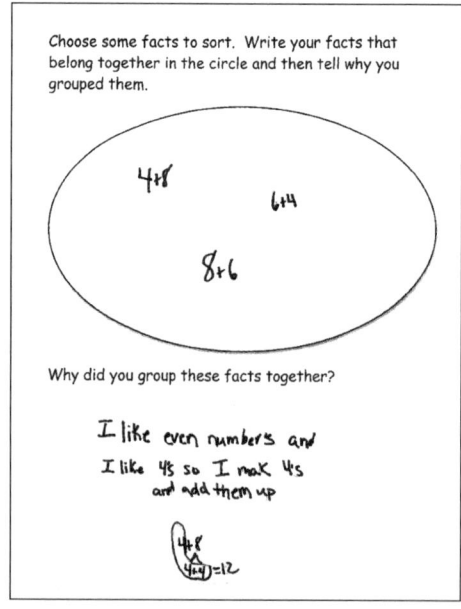

Fig. 3.4. A student's grouping of addition expressions and explanation for her sorting

This student-derived strategy incorporates an interesting method for thinking about these facts as alike. By using units of 4, this student was well on her way to understanding the power of multiplication. Her ability to decompose the value of each number into groups of 4, because she "liked 4," allowed her to make sense of addition facts with addends of 4 or multiples of 4 and use a fairly sophisticated grouping strategy. You might consider how you could work with such a student to extend this strategy to other problems.

Reflect 3.4 focuses on a sorting that relies on a different "rule." Let the questions guide your exploration of the rationale for this grouping of addition expressions before examining the student's work, shown in figure 3.5.

Reflect 3.4

A student grouped the following expressions:

$$9 + 7 \quad 4 + 6 \quad 6 + 8 \quad 3 + 5$$

Why might the student have grouped these combinations of addends together?

How does your explanation compare with the student's, given in the work in figure 3.5?

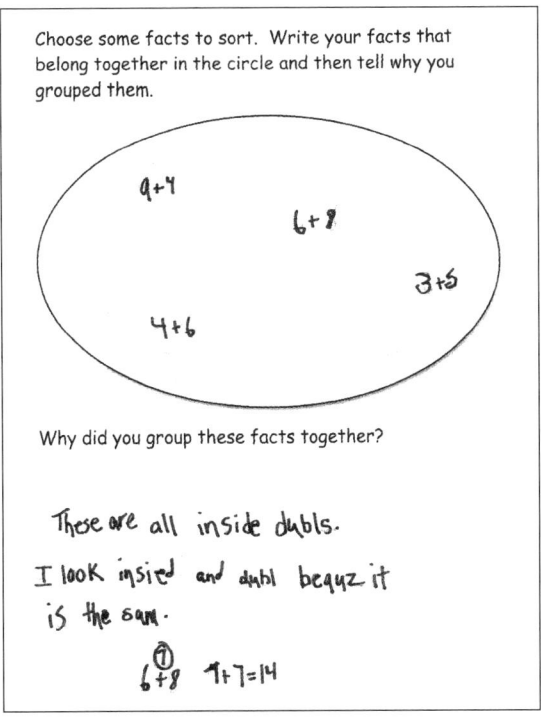

Fig. 3.5. A student's grouping of addition expressions and explanation for the sorting

The student who made this grouping noticed that the whole number that comes between the two whole number addends can be added to itself, or doubled, and the sum will be the same as the sum of the whole numbers below and above the "inside" number on a number line:

$$9 + 7 = 8 + 8 \quad \text{(number between 9 and 7 doubled)}$$

$$4 + 6 = 5 + 5 \quad \text{(number between 4 and 6 doubled)}$$

The student used the common name for the strategy behind the grouping: "inside doubles."

This very powerful insight demonstrates the student's ability to see relationships among seemingly unrelated facts. This student was using what might be described as a rudimentary averaging technique, perhaps applying a pattern noticed in work with manipulative materials. After making a stick of 5 snap cubes and a stick of 7 snap cubes, a child could take a cube from the 7-stick and move it to the 5-stick to create two sticks of 6 (see fig. 3.6).

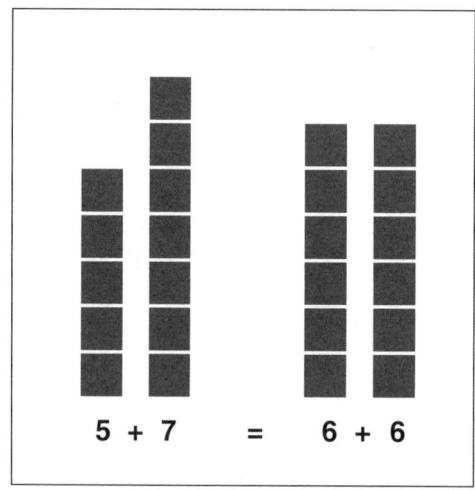

Fig. 3.6. Using snap cube "sticks" to compare 5 + 7 and 6 + 6

Students who identify this relationship and make this connection understand that many possibilities exist for representing a number, and they can compose and decompose numbers in a variety of ways. You could have such students represent the same concept on a number balance by placing 5 cubes and 7 cubes on one side of the balance and two sets of 6 cubes on the other side of the balance. You might then ask students to explain how or why the beam is balanced, with students comparing the basic fact combinations on the two sides of the balance to understand that the expressions 5 + 7 and 6 + 6 have the same value.

When students are exposed to all the common basic fact strategies in rapid succession, without opportunities to apply or make sense of them, they often become confused about how or when to apply a particular strategy, and instead they resort to a "count all" strategy. For example, students often develop misconceptions about the use of the "count on" strategy, which is best reserved for those facts that include an addend of 1, 2, or 3. Yet, students frequently apply this strategy to find any fact, even when using it is a laborious and time-consuming process. For instance, they may use it in determining the sum 8 + 9, counting on 9 more from 8.

Another misconception commonly held by students—and sometimes by teachers—is the notion that it is necessary to adhere rigidly to a specific strategy. For example, students might be taught that finding the sum 7 + 9 automatically calls for a "doubles plus 2" strategy and no other strategy, such as "make 10" or "inside doubles." When students think that they must use a specific strategy to find designated facts, they become overwhelmed by what they perceive as the need to choose the correct strategy. Frustrated, they may resort to drawing circles, counting on their fingers, or bobbing their heads to count by ones to the total. Allowing students time to sort, discuss, and explain how facts go together reduces misconceptions and ineffective use of strategies (O'Connell and SanGiovanni 2011).

Developing Understanding of Common Addition Strategies

After students have explored and shared strategies that they have developed on their own for determining the basic facts, you can present the common addition strategies explicitly, drawing on the student-derived strategies as examples or to help students make connections. Using student-derived strategies to demonstrate connections with the commonly used strategies can be the key to helping students develop more facility and fluency with strategies. After giving students many opportunities to connect strategies with basic facts, you can provide opportunities for them to select facts and practice various strategies. Students will naturally be drawn to particular strategies that make sense to them. Examples of these strategies may include "count on," "sum to 10" (or "make 10"), and "doubles" and associated strategies.

"Count on"

Examples of sums that students can find efficiently and effectively by using the "count on" strategy include 4 + 1, 6 + 3, 7 + 2, and so on. This strategy extends to obtaining sums such as 2 + 5, with the smaller addend first. Using this strategy, the student counts on from the higher number regardless of its placement in the expression. The realization that 2 + 5 and 5 + 2 result in the same sum leads to an important generalization that allows students to find the sum flexibly in either situation.

Students sometimes believe that they can use the "count on" strategy only if the smaller number is the second addend. This notion demonstrates their limited understanding of the commutative property.

"Sum to 10"

The "sum to 10" strategy, also called "make 10," applies to addition facts for sums of 10. Examples of sums that students can find by using the "sum to 10" strategy include 1 + 9, 2 + 8, 3 + 7, and so on. Teaching this strategy should include opportunities for students to develop ways to find all the combinations of whole numbers that sum to 10 and to identify a useful pattern in them. If students are asked to find only random combinations of addends that sum to 10, they often fail to connect *how* and *why* these facts go together. An important generalization or pattern that students should explicitly notice is that as one addend decreases by 1, the other addend increases by 1, and the sum remains 10. By discussing the pattern explicitly, among themselves and with the teacher, students recognize the logic in it and connect it with more complex computations. This work can also provide you with an opportunity to engage your students actively in two processes that are essential for learning mathematics with understanding at all levels, as emphasized in CCSSM's Standards for Mathematical Practice (NGA Center and CCSSO 2010, p. 8):

> 7. Look for and make use of structure.
> 8. Look for and express regularity in repeated reasoning.

Explicit teaching of the facts that sum to 10 builds on earlier work that students have done and ideas that they have developed by using ten frames. However, the "sum to 10" strategy is also helpful as students solve problems that involve sums larger than 10. Using decomposition and the flexibility developed by working with numbers, students can break numbers apart to redistribute quantities. For example, consider using decomposition and sums of 10 to determine 7 + 5, as shown in figure 3.7.

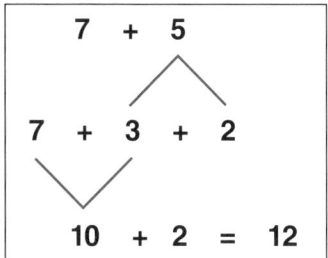

Fig. 3.7. Using the "sum to 10" strategy with
decomposition to determine 7 + 5 = 12

Figure 3.8 shows the work of a student who grouped together the addition expressions 9 + 4, 9 + 3, and 9 + 2. The student explained an invented "pretend it sums to 10" strategy that he used in making this grouping. This strategy is a student-derived modification and application of the "sum to 10" strategy.

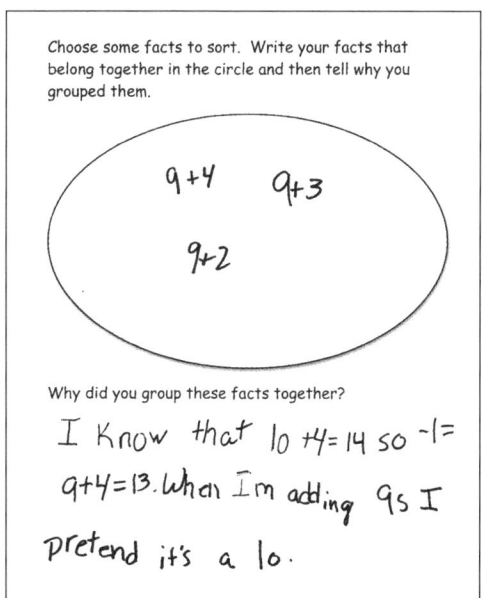

Fig. 3.8. A student's grouping of addition expressions
by "pretending" that a 9 is a 10

Explicit teaching of strategies for learning and retaining addition facts with sums of 10 can build effectively on prior work with ten frames while moving the students to develop compensation strategies that become extremely useful when they begin working with multi-digit numbers. For example, in adding 37 + 48, students might think about the sum by applying a compensation strategy that they learned in mastering basic facts related to sums of 10, as shown in figure 3.9.

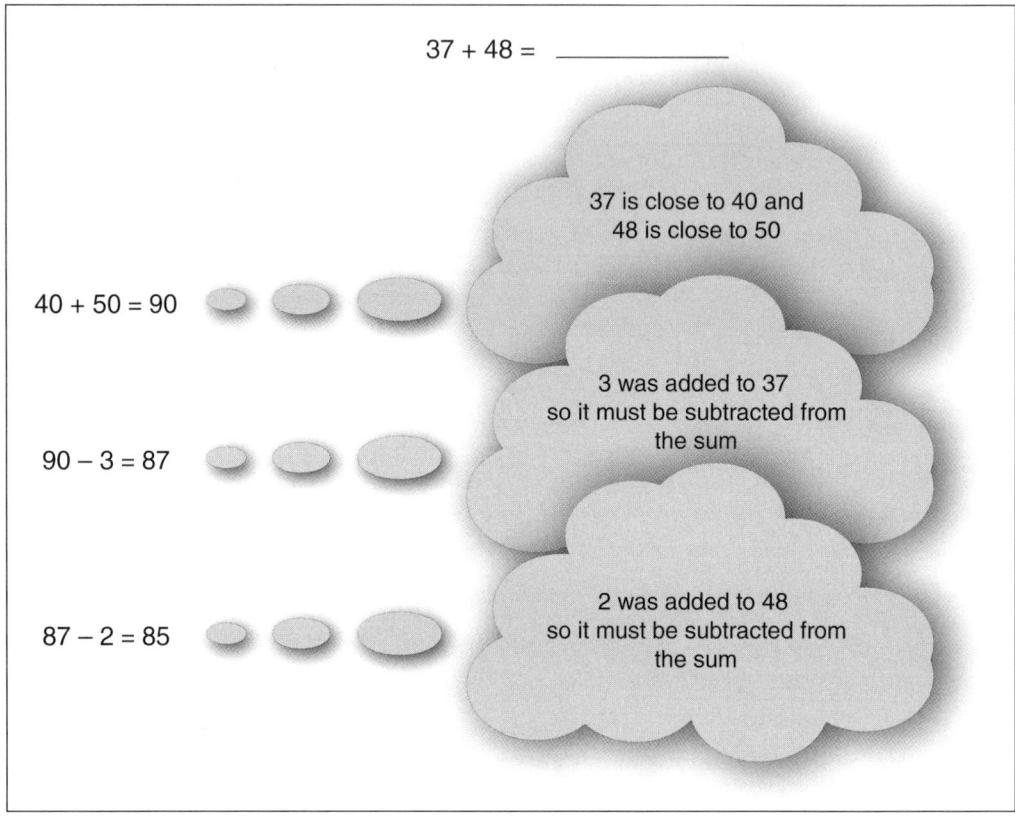

$37 + 48 =$ _____

37 is close to 40 and
48 is close to 50

$40 + 50 = 90$

3 was added to 37
so it must be subtracted from
the sum

$90 - 3 = 87$

2 was added to 48
so it must be subtracted from
the sum

$87 - 2 = 85$

Fig. 3.9. Using a compensation strategy to find $37 + 48 = 85$

When students use compensation, they substitute numbers that are easy to work with (decades, in the example in fig. 3.9), and then they add or subtract to compensate for the changes that they made. The use of this strategy illustrates students' proficiency in working flexibly with numbers, thinking of relationships between the addends and the sum, and applying a variation of the "sum to 10" strategy.

"Doubles" and associated strategies

The doubles facts include all the facts that have two addends that are the same quantity, such as $2 + 2 = 4$, $3 + 3 = 6$, $4 + 4 = 8$, $5 + 5 = 10$, and so on. Although children still have to memorize the doubles facts, once students have developed facility with them, these facts provide an anchor for other facts.

Students derive facts about "near doubles" from known doubles. They use a double to decompose one of the addends in a near double to assist in determining the new sum. Typically, these are addition problems that are associated with adding or subtracting 1 or 2 from a double. For example, figure 3.10 shows how a student might find the sum 4 + 6 by thinking of 4 + 6 as a double 4 plus 2. Alternatively, the student could derive this sum by thinking of it as a double 6 minus 2.

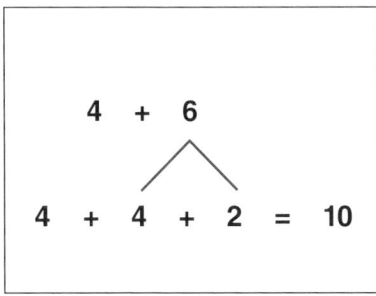

Fig. 3.10. Applying a "double + 2" strategy

Developing Understanding of Common Subtraction Strategies

Often young students approach subtraction through a "take away" model. They dutifully remove counters in a physical representation, pull apart a length of rods, or cover up pictures to find out what is remaining and then count to find the "answer," or the *difference*, in the language of subtraction.

Unfortunately, a "take away" strategy can be overgeneralized. Not all subtraction situations involve taking away, and teaching students to read or interpret the subtraction sign as "take away" can be misleading and cause long-term confusion. In teaching subtraction strategies, the concept of comparison becomes very helpful, and a "compare" strategy becomes useful and efficient. Careful attention to the meaningful development of subtraction strategies is the key to retention.

You can teach strategies for learning and retaining subtraction facts in the same sequence as addition strategies, beginning with student-derived strategies and then moving gradually to the common subtraction strategies while making explicit connections with the students' strategies. You can facilitate your students' understanding of strategies for subtraction facts by providing opportunities for them to connect their understanding of addition with their emerging understanding of subtraction.

Several strategies are particularly valuable for bridging from student-derived strategies to common subtraction strategies. In the following examples, questioning replaces simply stating or "telling" a strategy and serves to facilitate students' understanding of the strategy. After posing questions to support their understanding, showing students how the strategy works comes next, followed by giving them opportunities to use it. By presenting examples and using questions to bridge from unique student thinking to common strategies and ways of making sense of them, you can support reasoning that will in turn enhance retention.

"Think addition"

Students often use the "think addition" strategy naturally and unconsciously when subtracting, particularly when teachers or others encourage them to look at the relationship of the known part to the whole, or total. For example, when your students are finding the difference 12 – 9, you can ask questions to prompt them to "think addition":

- "How many more is 12 than 9?"

- "How many less is 9 than 12?"

- "How could you use addition to find the answer?"

- "How could you use the 'count on' strategy to find the difference?"

Compare the power of the "think addition" strategy with that of the "take away" strategy in the case of 12 – 9. Students who "think addition" focus on the relationship between the quantities, whereas students using the idea of "take away" might make or draw a set of 12 items, then laboriously cross off or remove 9 of them, and then count the remaining items in the set. By contrast, the "think addition" strategy encourages students to compare the two values. You might make, or suggest that your students make, a length of 9 cubes and a length of 12 cubes, and then ask, "How many more is this than that?"

Although the strategy of drawing or making a set of 12 items and then removing 9 of them is not mathematically incorrect, its use often demonstrates a naïve understanding that does not support students' development of more complex subtraction ideas or retention of them. Offering students the "take away" approach as the only model of subtraction misleads them because this approach does not accurately represent, and cannot reasonably be associated with, the intended actions or situations in all contextualized problems.

"Down over 10"

Students' experience with ten frames can help them see the power of using 10 as a benchmark in subtracting in the same way that it serves as a benchmark in addition.

You can facilitate this understanding by having your students solve a sequence of problems (Van de Walle et al. 2014). First, give them a set of subtraction problems like the following, in which a single-digit number is subtracted from a number that is 10 greater than itself:

$$15 - 5 = \square \qquad 16 - 6 = \square \qquad 12 - 2 = \square \qquad 14 - 4 = \square \qquad 13 - 3 = \square$$

Ask the students to tell you what they notice about all the problems. Students should respond that the difference is always equal to 10. Be sure to have them explain why each subtraction results in a difference of 10.

Next, modify the problems to increase each one-digit number by 1, and ask the students to solve the new problems:

$$15 - 6 = \square \qquad 16 - 7 = \square \qquad 12 - 3 = \square \qquad 14 - 5 = \square \qquad 13 - 4 = \square$$

Pose questions to motivate the students to think about the "down over 10" strategy:

- "Could you use the pattern that you noticed in the first set of problems to solve the problems in the this set? How?"
- "How does thinking about 10 help you subtract?"
- "Could you use 10 as a benchmark to help you subtract? How?"

As students explore the patterns that they find as they compare the two sets of problems, they should notice that in solving the problems in the second set, they are always subtracting 1 more than the digit in the ones place, whereas in the previous set, the subtraction always involved subtracting the same digit in the ones place. Thus, students might generalize that each subtraction in the second set results in 1 less than 10, or 9.

"Take from 10"

Another strategy, "take from 10," builds on whole number combinations that sum to 10. Once again, you can support your students' understanding of this strategy by presenting the facts carefully and asking questions to stimulate their thinking.

For example, you might first ask students to brainstorm to come up with all the pairs of one-digit numbers that sum to 10. Record their addend pairs in a pattern, with the first addends increasing by 1 each time and the second addends decreasing by 1, or vice versa. If you record the addend pairs in a logical pattern, students can make conceptual connections by inspecting the pattern that the combinations create. Ask students to think about how they might use the sums of 10 to solve the following subtraction problems:

$$13 - 8 = \square \qquad 15 - 8 = \square \qquad 17 - 9 = \square \qquad 12 - 8 = \square$$

In the case of $13 - 8 = \square$, for instance, you might say, "I want to think about using what I know about the combinations to 10. I can use both the 'count on' strategy and combinations of 10 to help me think about how to add up from 8 to 13. I know $8 + 2 = 10$. I want to get to 13, so I need to count on 3 more: $10 + 3 = 13$. Therefore, $13 - 8 = 5$."

You have probably discovered that your students will sometimes surprise you with strategies that they derive on their own even when you are presenting common strategies that you think they might use effectively. Or they may recognize or develop a particular known strategy in a way that is different from the process that you anticipated. Although students may be using their own strategies to subtract, you should encourage them to explain and connect their methods with concrete, pictorial, and abstract representations.

"Compare" and "part–whole"

Reflect 3.5 probes the reasoning of a student who grouped the subtraction expressions $8 - 4$, $12 - 6$, and $14 - 7$. Consider possible reasoning for this grouping before examining the student's work, shown in fig. 3.11.

Reflect 3.5

On the sorting task, one student grouped the following subtraction expressions:

$$8 - 4 \qquad 12 - 6 \qquad 14 - 7$$

What strategy might the student have used to see these expressions as alike? Examine the student's work, as shown in figure 3.11.

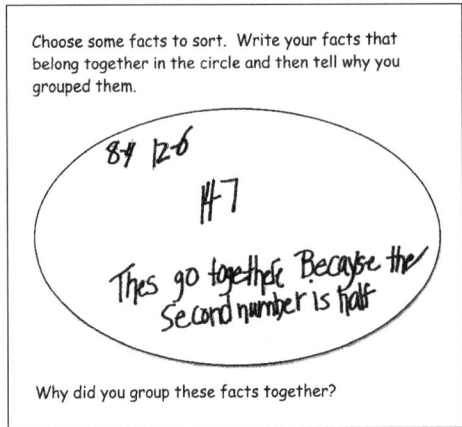

Choose some facts to sort. Write your facts that
belong together in the circle and then tell why you
grouped them.

8̸ 12̶6

14̸7

Thes go togethre Becayse the
second nanber is half

Why did you group these facts together?

Fig. 3.11. A student's grouping of subtraction expressions and explanation for the sorting

In grouping these subtraction expressions, this student saw a powerful relationship between the whole and the part, and the strategy that he developed not only makes sense but also demonstrates his understanding of the "compare" relationship. The student used this inherent relationship among the numbers in a subtraction problem and noticed that in these cases, the second number and the difference are both half of the whole given by the first number. Perhaps the student knew the "doubles" strategy and was applying this understanding to these subtraction facts. You might encourage such a student to use length models or tape diagrams to demonstrate further evidence of his or her thinking. By creating models for each value, the student could compare and clearly see the concept of "half" and even relate it back to the "doubles" strategy.

Reinforcing Strategies by Critiquing the Reasoning of Others

We presented students in second grade with a different task that is also beneficial in revealing misconceptions in their understanding of basic fact strategies. This task shows them another student's—in this case, a fictitious student's—choice of expressions to group together and asks them about the student's possible reasoning in linking two sums.

> **Task: Jose's Sorting of Sums**
>
> Jose said that he decided to put these two facts together. Do you agree that they belong together? Why or why not?
>
> 6 + 5   and   6 + 6

A classic misconception that might emerge as students work on this task is the notion that the grouping rests on the number 6—the number that the expressions have in common. A student might reason that the fictitious student put these expressions together simply because they both include an addend of 6. You might point out that yes, they both include 6, but how might this help someone add 6 + 5 or 6 + 6 quickly and efficiently?

Critically examining one another's ideas or the reasoning of fictitious students is an effective way for students to analyze and make sense of student-derived and teacher-taught strategies. Deciding whether they agree or disagree and then explaining how their own reasoning aligns or diverges from that thinking also reveals evidence of their critical thinking while engaging them in an essential mathematics process identified in the Standards for Mathematical Practice (NGA Center and CCSSO 2010, pp. 6–7):

3. Construct viable arguments and critique the reasoning of others.

Having students analyze another student's work can thus provide them with a powerful experience, increasing their conceptual understanding of the strategies. It can also be a revealing activity for you. Figure 3.12 shows two students' work on the task Jose's Sorting of Sums. Examine the two students' work and respond to the questions in Reflect 3.6.

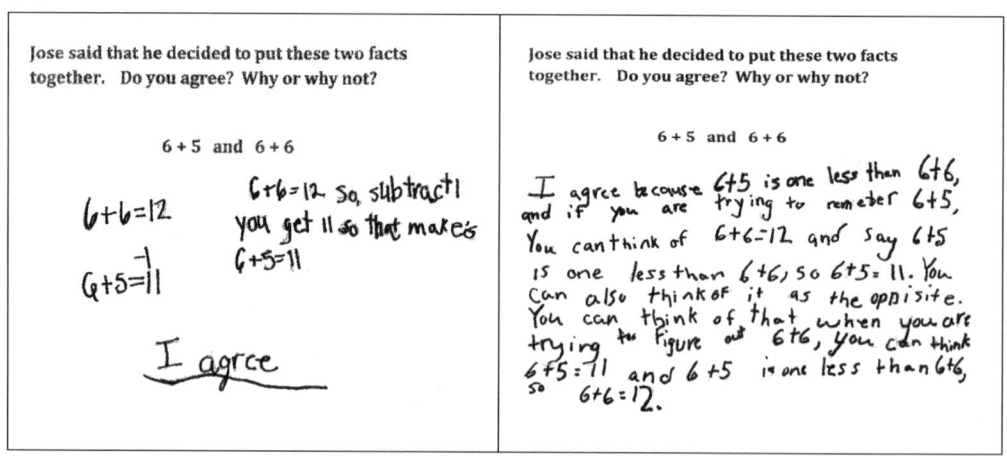

Fig. 3.12. Two students' thinking about Jose's grouping of 6 + 5 and 6 + 6

Reflect 3.6

Both students whose work is shown in figure 3.12 agreed with the decision of the fictitious student, Jose, to group 6 + 5 and 6 + 6 together.

Does their agreement indicate that both had attained the same level of critical thinking? Why or why not?

How did these two students support their agreement with Jose? What evidence did they give?

What might be the next instructional step to extend the understanding of each of these students?

Using Strings to Strengthen Understanding and Skill

Often in solving problems, students approach each pair of numbers individually without making the important connections that link the additions or subtractions. Finding the connections can allow them to streamline their problem solving by applying appropriate strategies and facts as they go. Although a one-by-one approach to problems does not constitute a misconception on the part of students, it often prohibits them from developing fluency. By contrast, working on addition and subtraction problems in "strings" can promote fluency.

Strings are sequences of problems that students can link through a strategy or pattern. After solving the first problem in a set, students can make connections and use similar processes or facts to solve subsequent problems, establishing other facts as they work. Typically, students obtain and establish the facts one at a time. After adding or subtracting to obtain one fact, they are given time to consider this fact and how they determined it as they add or subtract two new numbers, revealing the next fact in the string. Students share their ideas about the relationships that they find, record solutions, and use that information to solve the next problem, obtaining the next fact in the string. Recording the students' thinking for each fact in the string can help students make connections. Reflect 3.7 provides an opportunity to examine a string and consider how students might use strategies and links to solve the problems in it.

Reflect 3.7

Examine the following three sums:

$$9 + 7 = \square \qquad 8 + 7 = \square \qquad 8 + 9 = \square$$

Think about the connections that students could make from one sum to the next as they establish the first fact in the string and apply their reasoning and methods to the next fact. How might they use the information from their process of obtaining the preceding sum to obtain the next sum?

Figure 3.13 shows students' use of decomposing and recomposing to solve the problems in the string given in Reflect 3.7. In this example, students use a "break apart" strategy combined with a "make 10" strategy.

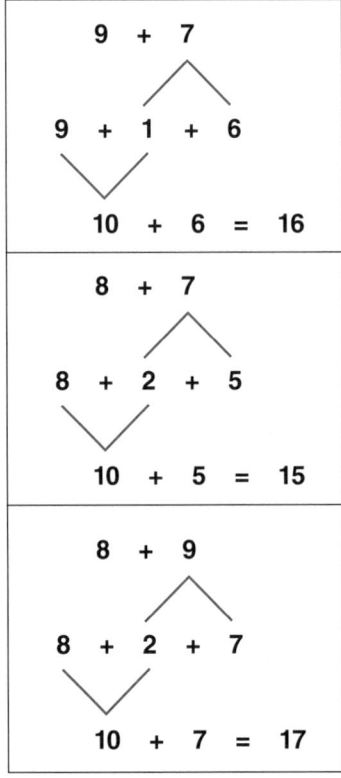

Fig. 3.13. A string of facts established by making connections and applying known facts and the "break apart" and "make 10" strategies

Using strings of problems to establish and reinforce related facts and fact strategies engages students in understanding the relationship of one fact to another. Students might use derived facts, decomposition, and place value strategies to solve each problem in the string. The reasoning used in solving problem strings can be apparent when students illustrate and share how they decompose numbers. If your students decompose numbers in unusual or inefficient ways, you can provide more experiences for them to decompose while working with concrete materials.

Developing Fluency

The Draft Progressions developed for kindergarten and kindergarten–grade 5 by the Common Core State Standards Writing Team (2011) define *fluency* as "fast and accurate" recall and use of basic facts (p. 18). Thus, fluency is similar to *automaticity*, as described by Baroody, Bajway, and Eiland (2009). Automaticity is the ability to recall answers with both speed and accuracy at an unconscious level. What is "fast and accurate" differs, depending on the grade level and individual student. Once students have a conceptual understanding of the common fact strategies and can identify, sort, and use both fact strategies and known and derived facts, they can work with retention techniques to develop fluency.

Building on their prior work, students can develop quick fact recall by using their own or common strategies to promote their retention. Van de Walle, Karp, and Bay-Williams (2013) devised the Spin, Circle, and Solve activity to support students' development of fact fluency. A slightly adapted version of this recall-reinforcing activity follows.

Spin, Circle, and Solve

Give your students a sheet with ten to twenty one-digit addition problems, and then have a student spin a "strategy spinner" like that in figure 3.14 to identify a particular strategy, such as "make 10" or "doubles," as the focus for this memory session. (The spinner shown is just one possible strategy spinner for Spin, Circle, and Solve; you can make a spinner that includes particular strategies that you are working on with your students.)

After the students have selected the strategy, they should circle all the problems on their sheet that they could solve by using that strategy—but they should not solve them yet.

Next, the students should have a short period of time, such as three minutes, to solve those problems—and those only—that they have circled.

The students should discuss their work to wrap up each Spin, Circle, and Solve session.

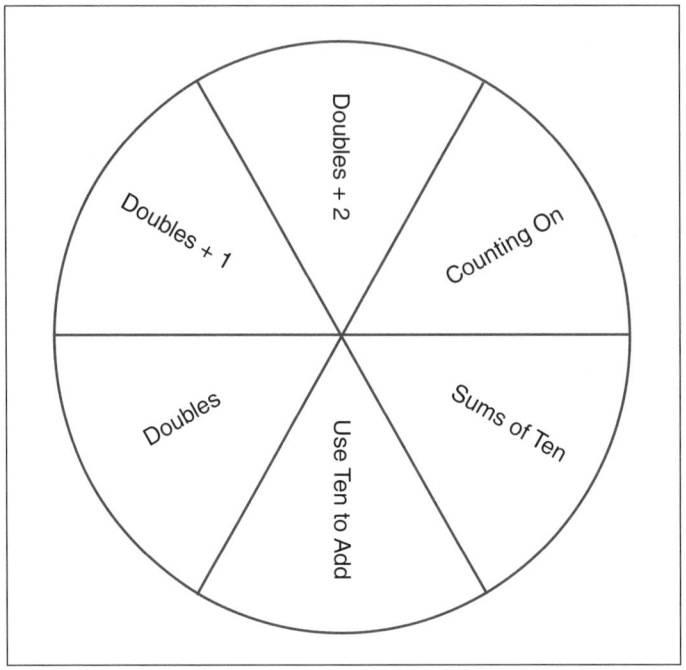

Fig. 3.14. A strategy spinner for playing a version of the Spin, Circle, and Solve activity, adapted from Van de Walle, Karp, and Bay-Williams (2013)

By separating circling and solving as distinct steps, you will divide the work into two essential components: identifying strategies and finding solutions. This two-part practice will help remind students to focus on a strategy first and on speed or fluency second.

Students often enjoy the surprise and fun of using a spinner to choose the strategy for this fluency work, and you can systematically add strategies to the mix as your students become more confident and efficient. Students can progress at their own rate as they make connections and build from known facts to develop fluency.

Figure 3.15 shows a set of ten addition problems, with six circled. Pause to consider the possible rationale for the circling, as directed in Reflect 3.8.

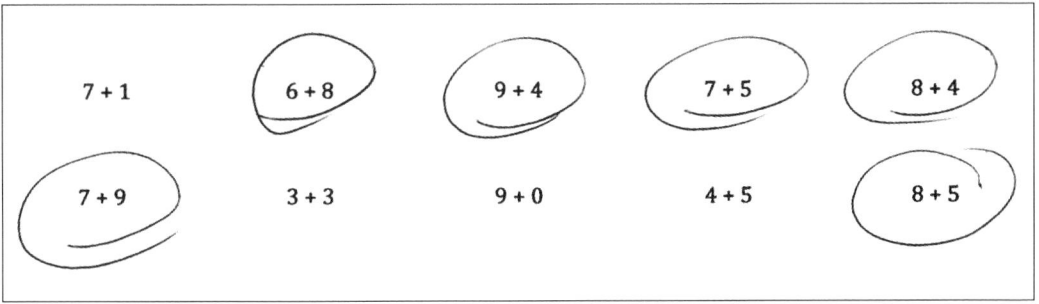

Fig. 3.15. A set of problems for Spin, Circle, and Solve, with six problems circled

Reflect 3.8

Look at the circled problems in the problem set for Spin, Circle, and Solve in figure 3.15.

What strategy do you think students might have spun on their strategy spinner for this session of the activity?

How might a student approach solving the circled problems?

You can help your students develop fluency by introducing other activities and games as well. Students enjoy and need many opportunities for repetition, and games provide the perfect forum for stress-free practice. You can also differentiate the games to suit your students' needs by increasing or decreasing the level of difficulty. After you teach a game, your students can play it during center time, at a learning station, or as part of a homework assignment. Three possible games appear below:

Game 1. Strategy-Solve-Pairs

Students play in groups of 2 to 4.

Materials: Basic fact cards (and counters if the students need them).

Set up: Place addition and subtraction basic fact cards facedown in a pile on the table. (Modify the game if you wish by using only addition cards or only subtraction cards.)

Goal: Be the first player to get five pairs of basic fact cards.

Rules:
1. Players take turns turning over basic fact cards one at a time from the pile. Each player must name a strategy that he or she can use to find the sum or difference on the card, and then the player should find it. If the player gives the correct answer, he or she keeps the card. If the answer is incorrect, the player must place the card at the bottom of the pile.

2. Players continue taking turns in this way, identifying strategies, solving problems, and collecting cards until a player turns over a card with a problem that he or she can solve by applying a strategy that he or she has already used. Then, if the player solves the problem correctly, he or she can put the new card with the earlier card to make a pair. For example, a player who has drawn the card showing 6 + 6 might have solved that problem by using a "doubles" strategy. If that player later draws the card showing 4 + 4, he or she can use the strategy again to make a pair.

3. The first player to make five pairs wins the game.

Game 2. Addition Challenge

Students play in pairs.

Materials: A standard deck of playing cards with face cards removed (and counters if the students need them).

Set up: Shuffle the cards, and deal them facedown into two piles in front of the players.

Goal: Be the player with more cards at the end of the game.

Rules:
1. Both players turn a card face up on the table at the same time. This action constitutes a "round."

2. The first player to say the correct sum of the numbers on the two cards wins the pair of cards. If the first player to speak gives an incorrect sum, the other player can challenge it and win the cards if he or she gives the correct sum.

3. Play continues for a predetermined number of rounds, and the player who has more cards at the end of the final round wins the game.

Game 3. Ring Facts

Students play in groups of 2 to 6.

Materials: A Ring Facts game board for each player (fig. 3.16 shows a game board in play; Appendix 3 at More4U includes a template for a blank board); one to two sets of basic fact cards (addition and subtraction); smiley-face stickers or buttons for the players to use to mark their preselected numbers on their game boards.

Set up: Distribute game boards and stickers or buttons to all players, and stack basic fact cards facedown on each table, within everyone's reach.

Goal: Be the first player to draw rings around five preselected numbers on a game board after those numbers have occurred as sums or differences for problems on basic fact cards.

Rules:
1. Each player chooses five numbers to "ring" on his or her game board and puts a sticker or button on the corner of each of those numbered squares.

2. Players take turns turning over cards, with each player displaying the problem on his or her card and reading it aloud to the other players. All the players find the sum or difference to complete the fact, and then each player looks to see whether he or she marked that sum or difference on his or her game board. If so, the player "rings" the sum by drawing a circle around it. For example, if player 1 turns over the problem 4 + 1, all the players find the sum, 5, and then look to see whether they preselected 5. If they did, they "ring" the sum.

3. The first player to ring all five previously marked numbers wins the game.

1	2	3	4	5 ☺
6 ☺	7	8 ☺	9	10
11	12	13	14	15
16	17	18 ☺	19	20 ☺

Fig. 3.16. A Ring Facts game board with five numbers marked for play

Summary: Learners, Curriculum, Instruction, and Assessment

Effective teaching of basic fact strategies incorporates rich knowledge of learners, curriculum, instructional strategies, and assessment. You must draw on knowledge from all these areas to help your students make the transition to fluency. As this chapter has emphasized, learners need to have opportunities to derive and use invented strategies and make sense of and connect known or taught strategies with the concepts of addition and subtraction. Understanding your students' misconceptions and perceptions about how facts fit together gives you powerful insights into their reasoning, and you can use these in designing and implementing tasks that will offer your students meaningful opportunities to develop and use these strategies. This approach also has the benefit of emphasizing the strategy over the answer, shifting the focus away from solutions.

Task selection is a crucial curricular tool with the potential to enhance learners' abilities to make sense of the strategies, learn from other students, and develop their own reasoning about how and why particular facts are related. This chapter has also discussed student misconceptions related to basic fact strategies. Assessing student understanding of basic facts goes far beyond determining how many facts students can supply in a set time period. By understanding how students think about the facts that they are learning, you can design better tasks, ask more productive questions, and develop targeted lessons that uncover student misunderstandings.

Assigning and discussing student work, identifying or developing assessment tasks, selecting or designing curricular materials, and engaging throughout in related decision making are crucial components of your work of developing your students' knowledge of basic facts and fact strategies. Although the components are many, you can think of this work as a fairly straightforward three-stage process:

1. Ask students to explore, derive, and explain their own strategies.

2. Use the students' strategies to increase understanding for all students through an examination of their efficiency and practicality.

3. Have students analyze other students' strategies either to solidify their own conceptual understanding or to broaden their own limited use of strategies.

This chapter has focused on the use of student-derived strategies as a vehicle for increasing both conceptual understanding of basic fact strategies and procedural fluency. A focus on student-derived strategies can guide your selection of tasks, response to the student-derived strategies, and decisions about when to introduce common strategies. Discussing and probing students' work can guide you in developing fact strategies explicitly to move your students past the "count all" strategy for addition or the "take away" strategy for subtraction. When students derive their own strategies and examine other students' strategies, they begin to notice and apply patterns (Crespo, Kyriakides, and McGee 2006).

Throughout this process, your role in responding to your students' ideas is crucial. This approach will challenge your students to use reasoning to understand and retain the basic facts while also challenging you to pay careful attention to the unique thinking of your students. You must be "present" in your teaching and respond to students' ideas by asking important questions to enhance their critical thinking. By having students examine others' strategies, you can help them learn from and adapt their own ideas and increase their own knowledge of strategies. Finally, by using a variety of practice activities that focus on developing automaticity through strategy work, you can develop your students' fluency while you are differentiating instruction for each learner.

Conclusion

To develop full conceptual understanding of strategies and fluency with basic facts, students need to have time to wrestle with the connections of the facts with physical models, strategies, and other facts. In your long-term planning, consider how you could develop the techniques and strategies over the course of the entire academic year. Teaching a strategy a day for a couple of weeks and then timing students on their use of each one does not develop the fluency that they need.

Students must have many experiences in devising their own strategies to develop conceptual understanding of basic addition and subtraction facts.

Of course, this kind of instruction takes time, planning, and patience while students progress from inefficient and laborious strategies to more common and efficient ones. Once your students have had multiple opportunities to construct their own strategies, you can introduce new ones, connecting what they have developed with known strategies. Students also need many opportunities to discuss and analyze these strategies by sorting facts and comparing strategies that they and other students use.

After helping your students to develop this repertoire of strategies, you can encourage them to develop fluency by continuing the important work of using strategies, and you can gradually develop both their speed and accuracy by using games and carefully implementing timing techniques that focus on student self-improvement. Careful monitoring of student strategies and planning for development and differentiation are the keys to long-term understanding and retention of basic facts.

into

practice

Chapter 4
Understanding Multi-Digit Addition and Subtraction

Big Idea 2
The mathematical foundations for understanding computational procedures for addition and subtraction of whole numbers are the properties of addition and place value.

Essential Understanding 2c
Place-value concepts provide a convenient way to compose and decompose numbers to facilitate addition and subtraction concepts.

Essential Understanding 2d
Properties of addition are central in justifying the correctness of computational algorithms.

Students use what they have learned in previous years as they begin to add and subtract multi-digit numbers. They must either recall facts or use strategies to find sums of one-digit numbers, and they must understand place value to make sense of two-digit and three-digit numbers. However, when students begin adding and subtracting multi-digit numbers, their fluency with facts and understanding of place value are often limited. Identifying the sources of your students' difficulties carefully and correctly can be very valuable as you build their conceptual understanding of the big ideas of addition and subtraction and work to develop their fluency with computational algorithms.

This chapter highlights important ideas related to learners, curricular goals, instructional strategies, and assessment that can assist you in transforming your students' knowledge into formal mathematical ideas related to addition and subtraction of multi-digit numbers. Analyzing specific examples of mathematical tasks

Common Core State Standards for Mathematics

Related to the Big Idea and Essential Understandings for Chapter 4

Grade 1 (1.NBT.4–6)

Use place value understanding and properties of operations to add and subtract.

4. Add within 100, including adding a two-digit number and a one-digit number, and adding a two-digit number and a multiple of 10, using concrete models or drawings and strategies based on place value, properties of operations, and/or the relationship between addition and subtraction; relate the strategy to a written method and explain the reasoning used. Understand that in adding two-digit numbers, one adds tens and tens, ones and ones; and sometimes it is necessary to compose a ten.

5. Given a two-digit number, mentally find 10 more or 10 less than the number, without having to count; explain the reasoning used.

6. Subtract multiples of 10 in the range 10–90 from multiples of 10 in the range 10–90 (positive or zero differences), using concrete models or drawings and strategies based on place value, properties of operations, and/or the relationship between addition and subtraction; relate the strategy to a written method and explain the reasoning used.

Grade 2 (2.NBT.5–9)

Use place-value understanding and properties of operations to add and subtract.

5. Fluently add and subtract within 100 using strategies based on place value, properties of operations, and/or the relationship between addition and subtraction.

6. Add up to four two-digit numbers using strategies based on place value and properties of operations.

7. Add and subtract within 1000, using concrete models or drawings and strategies based on place value, properties of operations, and/or the relationship between addition and subtraction; relate the strategy to a written method. Understand that in adding or subtracting three-digit numbers, one adds or subtracts hundreds and hundreds, tens and tens, ones and ones; and sometimes it is necessary to compose or decompose tens or hundreds.

8. Mentally add 10 or 100 to a given number 100–900, and mentally subtract 10 or 100 from a given number 100–900.

9. Explain why addition and subtraction strategies work, using place value and the properties of operations.

(National Governors Association Center for Best Practices and Council of Chief State School Officers [NGA Center and CCSSO] 2010, pp. 16, 19) and student thinking can help you develop your pedagogical content knowledge for teaching addition and subtraction of multi-digit numbers in grades 1–2 or give you ideas for helping other colleagues develop this knowledge.

Discussion in this chapter illustrates four themes based on research on how children learn to add and subtract multi-digit numbers:

1. Curricula and instruction should stress conceptual understanding and seek from the outset to build flexible application of multiple strategies. Studies indicate that such curricula and instruction lead to understanding that is deeper than, and procedural skill that is equivalent to but more fluent and flexible than, the corresponding understanding and skill achieved through approaches that initially stress mastery of procedures (Sarama and Clements 2009; Fuson and Kwon 1992; Hiebert and Wearne 1996; National Mathematics Advisory Panel 2008).

2. Emphasizing place value and working with students on mental math prior to introducing them to paper-and-pencil algorithms lead to enhanced conceptual understanding and procedural knowledge (Sarama and Clements 2009; Verschaffel, Greer, and de Corte 2007).

3. Most errors that students make on multi-digit addition and subtraction problems are the result of systematic "bugs" in their work (Sarama and Clements 2009; Hiebert and Wearne 1996), including failing to line up numbers properly or having a limited recall of facts.

4. Students need to continue to work with a variety of problem contexts that involve them in adding to, taking from, putting together, taking apart, and comparing, with unknowns in all positions (Verschaffel, Greer, and de Corte 2007).

Developing Strategies for Multi-Digit Addition

One of the major barriers to understanding the addition process is failing to connect the computational procedures for adding multi-digit numbers with place value. Big Idea 2 (Caldwell, Karp, and Bay-Williams 2011) suggests that multi-digit addition and subtraction involve the use of strategies based on concepts of place value and properties of operations. One of the first choices that you face as a teacher is how to present a task. Should you use a story problem? Would manipulative materials be useful, and if so, which ones? What numbers should you use? Should you write the numbers horizontally or vertically? The context, the models, the numbers, and the presentation of the numbers may lead students to consider different strategies for computation.

Designing, adapting, or selecting worthwhile assessment tasks, interpreting the responses of specific children, and making instructional decisions on the basis of what has happened in the classroom so far all call for specialized knowledge. For example, think about the questions in Reflect 4.1 as you consider the four assessment tasks for students in grades 1–2 presented in figure 4.1.

Reflect 4.1

Figure 4.1 shows four assessment tasks used with students in grades 1–2 as they were beginning to add two-digit numbers.

How might students approach each of these tasks?

What mathematical tools might you provide to help students solve these problems?

In what order might you use these tasks?

How might changing the numbers in the tasks affect their level of difficulty or the strategies that students might use?

Task A
Stickers come in packs of 10. A box of stickers holds 10 packs. Susie has 4 packs and 3 more stickers. Jose has 6 packs and 9 more stickers. How many stickers do they have in all?

Task B
Susie has 43 stickers. Jose has 69 stickers. How many stickers do they have in all?

Task C
43 + 69 = ?

Task D
$$\begin{array}{r} 43 \\ + 69 \\ \hline \end{array}$$

Fig. 4.1. Four two-digit addition tasks

Each of these tasks involves adding the same numbers, but tasks A and B provide a context, whereas tasks C and D do not. The story itself may suggest a type of model for students to use in solving the problem, as the three students' solutions in figure 4.2 illustrate. Use the questions in Reflect 4.2 to guide your examination of these first- and second-grade students' work on task A.

Reflect 4.2

Figure 4.2 shows three students' modeling to solve task A in figure 4.1. How are these first- and second-grade students' solutions alike, and how are they different?

What are the advantages and disadvantages of each type of manipulative used by the students?

Amy's solution
Amy made drawings to show the stickers that Susie and Jose had:

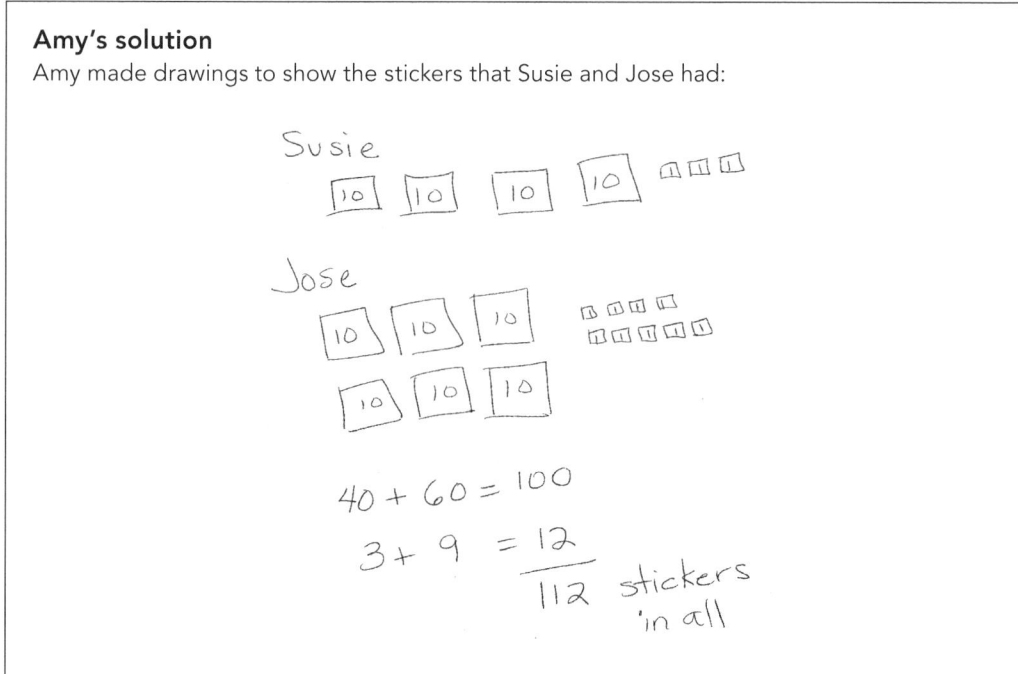

Fig. 4.2. Amy's, Ben's, and Sheila's modeling of task A in figure 4.1

Ben's solution

Ben's teacher distributed smiley-face stickers grouped in tens and ones; Ben arranged them as shown and then counted by tens and ones:

10	20	30	40	50	60	70	80	90	100		
1	2	3	4	5	6	7	8	9	10	11	12

112 stickers in all

Sheila's solution

Sheila used straws and made bundles of 10 to represent packs of stickers, with 10 bundles of 10 and 12 individual straws giving her 112 stickers:

Fig. 4.2. *Continued*

All three students used place value knowledge in representing and solving task A. Amy added tens and ones, Ben counted by tens and by ones, and Sheila made bundles of tens and ones. Each student began by considering the tens first and then the ones, proceeding in an order that is quite typical. Amy drew her own version of the problem; Ben and Sheila used materials provided by the teacher. Sheila used straws to make her own groups of tens and ones, a process that may have given her a better understanding of how place value affects addition, facilitating adding tens to tens and ones to ones. The stickers that Ben used were already grouped in tens and ones, arrangements that may be more suitable for students who have already acquired a solid understanding of place value than for students whose understanding is still developing. Ben's counting suggests that he may benefit from doing his own bundling rather than using pre-bundled materials provided by the teacher.

Task B in figure 4.1 presents the same context as task A and poses the same question: How many stickers do Susie and Jose have in all? This time, however, the information is different, with the task explicitly giving the total numbers of stickers that Susie and Jose have individually. Use the questions in Reflect 4.3 to guide your inspection of the two students' work shown in figure 4.3.

Reflect 4.3

Figure 4.3 shows the work of two second-grade students, Angel and Helen, on task B in figure 4.1.

How did each student use place value and properties of addition to help solve the problem?

Angel, the first student whose work is shown, solved the problem by working with an open number line.

What would an appropriate justification of Angel's thinking look like?

Angel's solution
Angel placed values on an open number line to add Susie's and Jose's stickers:

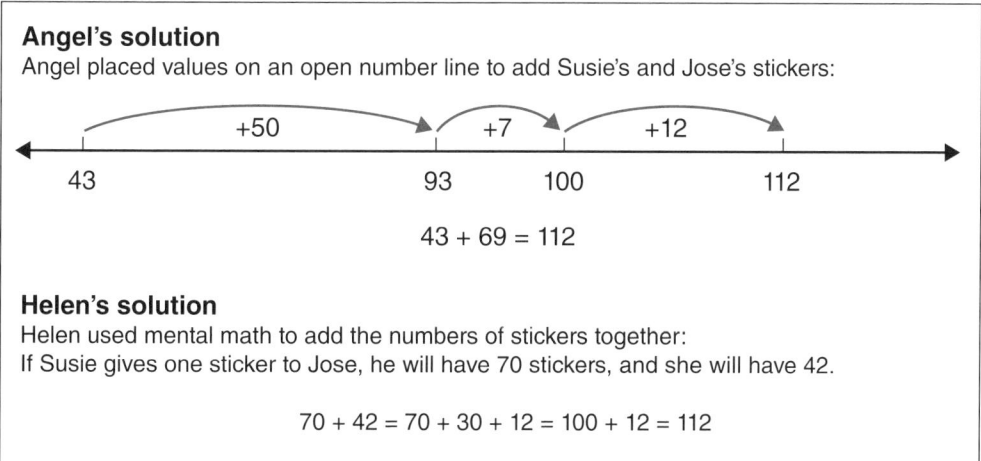

$$43 + 69 = 112$$

Helen's solution
Helen used mental math to add the numbers of stickers together:
If Susie gives one sticker to Jose, he will have 70 stickers, and she will have 42.

$$70 + 42 = 70 + 30 + 12 = 100 + 12 = 112$$

Fig. 4.3. Angel's and Helen's solutions for task B in figure 4.1

Both Angel and Helen broke the numbers apart (decomposition), flexibly using the associative and commutative properties to rearrange the addends. Both also used place value, appearing to understand that adding tens and ones separately is efficient. Angel began with one of the given numbers and then decomposed the second addend, breaking it apart so that it was easy to add to find the total. Helen used a compensation strategy, taking 1 away from one number and adding it to the other to get a multiple of 10, and then she decomposed the second number into tens and ones. Students in first and second grade should be able to explain their thinking, using numbers and pictures. For example, Angel might move from left to right on her number line, pointing to the parts of her drawing and saying, "I started with the first number, 43, and added 50, since it was easy to add. Then I had 93, and I needed 7 more to get to 100. Then I had added on 50 + 7 = 57, but I needed 69. So, 69 – 57 = 12 more. So the answer is 112."

Tasks C and D in figure 4.1 present the same addition problem as tasks A and B but without context. In these tasks, the problem is presented symbolically, with numerals and a plus sign. Task C gives the expression in horizontal form, and task D presents it in vertical form. Use the questions in Reflect 4.4 to guide your examination of the work of three second-grade students—Craig, Juan, and Fran—on these tasks, as shown in figure 4.4.

Reflect 4.4

Figure 4.4 shows work by three second-grade students on tasks C and D in figure 4.1. How are the students' solutions alike, and how are they different?

Craig and Juan arrived at the correct answer, but Fran did not. What error did Fran make?

How does the orientation—horizontal or vertical—of a problem affect students' thinking?

With a problem presented vertically, like task D, why might students be more comfortable working from left to right rather than from right to left?

What, if anything, can you tell about Craig's understanding of the equal sign?

Craig's solution
Craig solved task C by thinking about place value:

$$43 + 69 = 40 + 60 + 3 + 9 = 100 + 12 = 112$$

Juan's and Fran's solutions
Juan and Fran both approached task D by thinking about place value but arrived at different answers:

Juan	Fran
43	43
+69	+69
100	1012
+12	
112	

Fig. 4.4. Craig's solution to task C, and Juan's and Fran's solutions to task D

Craig, Juan, and Fran were all adding tens to tens and ones to ones. Craig and Juan both used the same solution strategy, and both obtained the correct answer. They were using the partial sums algorithm to add the numbers, although they recorded their work in different ways. Fran was trying to use a similar strategy but seems to have been thinking of the problem as two side-by-side one-digit problems, and thus she failed to combine the tens properly and arrived at a completely unreasonable answer.

A student like Fran might benefit from using the partial sums algorithm or working with problems in horizontal form. Doing so would encourage her to think about the magnitudes of the numbers. She might also benefit from using a variety of manipulative materials, such as base-ten blocks, to help her model and solve the problem or estimate where the answer might be situated on a number line (for example, between 100 and 200, 200 and 300, etc.).

All three students—Craig, Juan, and Fran—might have worked from left to right, starting with the tens place and then moving to the ones place. Working from left to right replicates the process that students use for reading, and having students proceed in this manner may be particularly helpful to emphasize when thinking about place value is important.

Developing Strategies for Multi-Digit Subtraction

Students often struggle with subtraction as a result of difficulties that they have in understanding the various contexts for subtraction and the inverse relationship between subtraction and addition. To use addition and subtraction successfully to solve a wide variety of story problems, students must understand and be able to shift flexibly from one meaning for these operations to another. These meanings include "add to," "take from," "put together," "take apart," and "compare." Reflect 4.5 offers an opportunity to think closely about contextual problems that invite these interpretations of addition or subtraction.

Reflect 4.5

Create story problems of varying types ("add to," "take from," "put together," "take apart," and "compare"), with the unknown in various positions, for the following problem:

$$702 - 458 = \square$$

Perhaps you created some problems like tasks A and B in figure 4.5, both of which present the same context and ask students to work with the same numbers but call on them to apply different interpretations of addition or subtraction. After reading the two problems, pause to examine them more closely, as Reflect 4.6 suggests.

Task A
Georgette has 702 stickers. She has 458 stickers left after she gives some to her friend, Annie. How many stickers did Georgette give to Annie?

Task B
Sam has 458 stickers. He buys some more stickers. Now he has 702 stickers. How many stickers did Sam buy?

Fig. 4.5. Two story problems of different types

Reflect 4.6

Write a number sentence for each of the story problems in figure 4.5.
How are your two number sentences alike? How are they different?

Because of the order of the actions in the two story problems, you might have used subtraction in your sentence for task A and addition in your sentence for task B. Or you might have used subtraction in both cases, writing the same number sentence each time: 702 – 458 = □. Figure 4.6 shows how two students who wrote an addition sentence for task B and a subtraction sentence for task A might have written values on an open number line and used them to solve these problems. After studying the work in the figure, pause to respond to the questions in Reflect 4.7 about the students' strategies.

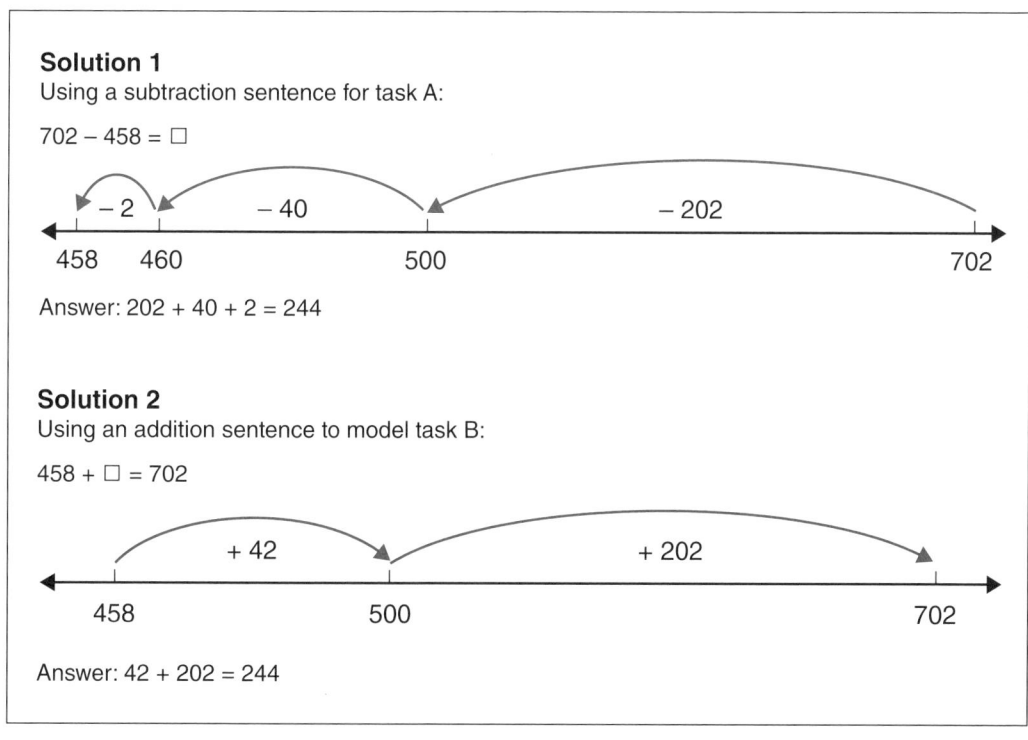

Solution 1
Using a subtraction sentence for task A:

702 – 458 = □

– 2   – 40   – 202
458   460   500   702

Answer: 202 + 40 + 2 = 244

Solution 2
Using an addition sentence to model task B:

458 + □ = 702

+ 42   + 202
458   500   702

Answer: 42 + 202 = 244

Fig. 4.6. Two students' number sentences and solutions for tasks A and B in figure 4.5

Reflect 4.7

Figure 4.6 shows two students' strategies for solving the tasks in figure 4.5.

How are the strategies alike? How are they different?

How does each strategy relate to the problem posed?

Is counting back more challenging than counting on to get the answer?

Both solution strategies in figure 4.6 use jumps marked on an open number line. The student who solved task A (solution 1) used subtraction jumps, and the student who solved task B (solution 2) used addition jumps, even though both students could have solved by subtracting 702 – 458. Note that in both solutions, the students began with the first number used in the statement of the problem—a very natural place to start. They then modeled the actions described in each problem to find the answer.

Other students might solve the same problems in different ways. Some might use mental math, and others might choose base-ten blocks. Allowing students to use a variety of methods accommodates individual differences in fact fluency and understanding of place value. However, you must be sure to connect the various strategies that your students use and encourage them to move toward more efficient strategies that are based on place value and the properties of addition. Figure 4.7 shows two other ways to solve the problem 702 – 458 = □ besides using the number line as in solution 1 in figure 4.6. Consider these two new solution strategies before responding to the questions in Reflect 4.8.

---

702 – 458 = □

Strategy A

I can add the same number to both numbers without changing the difference.

I will add 42 to both numbers so that I can subtract an even 500 from 744:

702 – 458 becomes 744 – 500
744 – 500 = 244

Fig. 4.7. Two more strategies for solving 702 – 458 = □

Strategy B

I can break the numbers apart by place values, starting on the left:

> 700 − 400 = 300
> 300 − 50 = 250
> 2 − 8 means I need to subtract 6.
> So 250 − 6 = 244

Fig. 4.7. Continued

Reflect 4.8

Compare strategies A and B in figure 4.7 for solving 702 − 458 = □.

Try using these strategies to solve 821 − 357 = □.

Do both strategies work equally well?

Would other strategies work for better for 821 − 357 = □?
For 702 − 458 = □?

The major benefit of allowing students to find their own ways of doing addition and subtraction problems is the development of number sense, fluency, and flexibility. Research suggests that students benefit from frequent opportunities to build adaptive expertise—learning to take into consideration the problem itself, the accuracy and speed of various strategies, and their own capabilities (Sarama and Clements 2009).

Moving toward the Traditional Algorithm

Working with base-ten blocks can move students toward the traditional algorithm for subtraction. Carefully structuring the use of the base-ten blocks is important, however, and can eliminate the confusion that some students otherwise experience when they encounter them in this context. Figure 4.8 illustrates one way of using base-ten blocks to model the same subtraction problem as before: 702 − 458 = □. The figure calls this method strategy C; Reflect 4.9 poses some follow-up questions for your consideration after you examine the strategy.

702 – 458 = □

Strategy C

I can use base-ten blocks. I will start with 7 hundreds and 2 units.

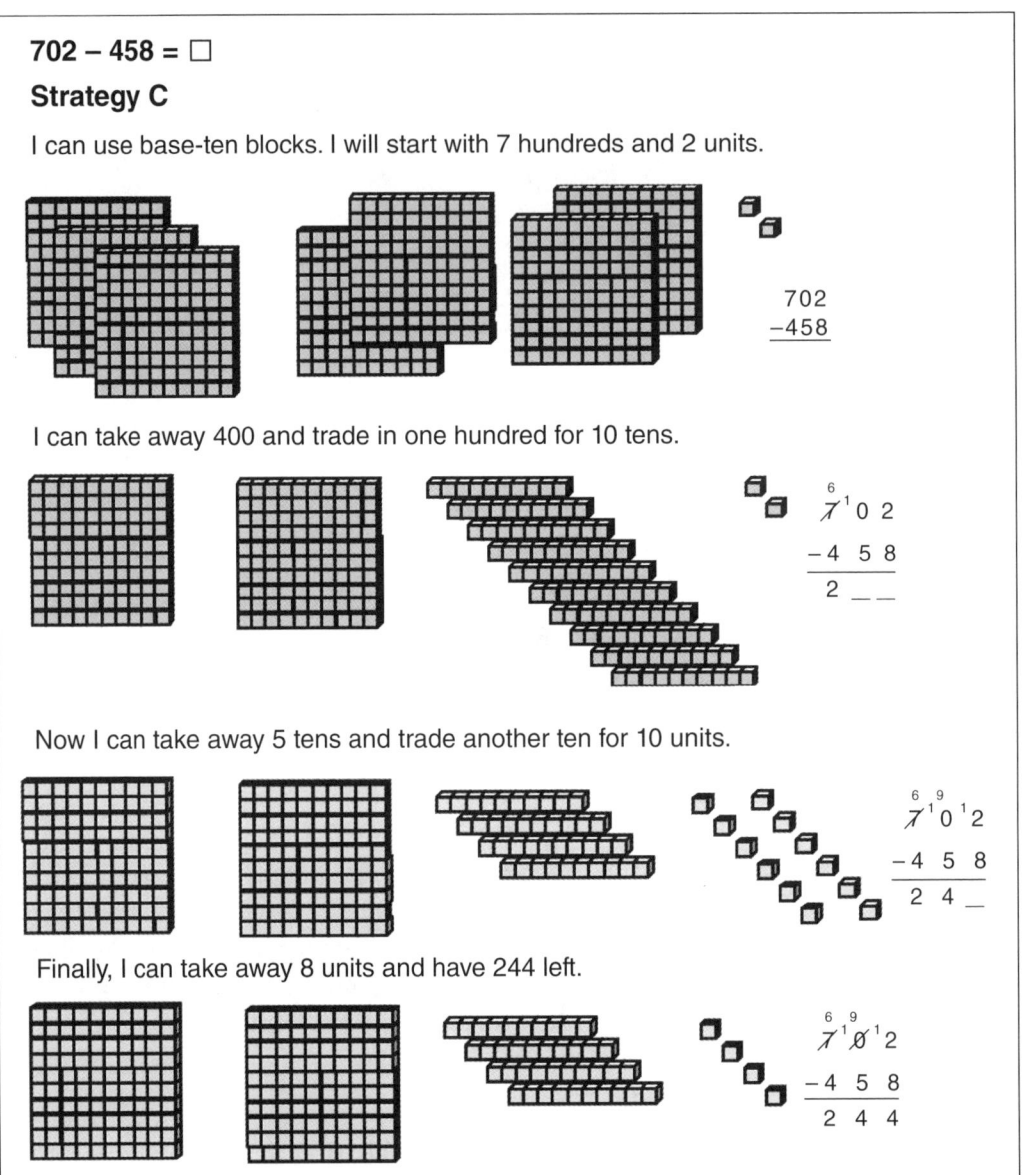

I can take away 400 and trade in one hundred for 10 tens.

Now I can take away 5 tens and trade another ten for 10 units.

Finally, I can take away 8 units and have 244 left.

Fig. 4.8. Using base-ten blocks to find 702 – 458 = □

Reflect 4.9

Can you identify a possible source of confusion in the strategy for solving 702 − 458 = □ with base-ten blocks presented in figure 4.8?

How might you help this student move toward use of the standard algorithm for subtraction?

Progressing through a Sequence of Tasks

Students often seem to understand how to add or subtract but become confused when the verbal directions, orientation (vertical or horizontal), the numbers, or the settings change. In selecting tasks for students, you must consider not only types of problems and appropriate models and contexts but also the actual numbers themselves. In some of the tasks presented previously in this chapter, the numbers promoted the use of particular strategies. The numbers used may also affect how difficult the problems are for students as well as what solution strategies they consider.

Reflect 4.10 probes the effect of the numbers on the level of difficulty of the problems presented in figure 4.9.

Reflect 4.10

Which of the problems in figure 4.9 do you think would be easiest for your students? Which would be most difficult? Why?

Should each of these types of problems be taught separately to students? Why or why not?

132	856	812	812	702	680	680
− 21	− 143	− 408	− 459	− 355	− 40	− 240

Fig. 4.9. Sequencing subtraction problems

Traditionally, elementary mathematics instruction has moved into three-digit subtraction after two-digit subtraction, perhaps beginning with problems involving subtracting a two-digit number from a three-digit number. For students using the standard algorithm, problems in which a zero appears in the tens place have generally been regarded as the most difficult type for students to solve and thus have been reserved for last. However, encouraging students to use reasoning and sense making in subtracting multi-digit numbers eliminates the need to adhere to the traditional sequence of tasks. For example, 812 – 408 becomes an easy subtraction for a student who thinks, "800 – 400 = 400, and 12 – 8 = 4, so the answer is 404." Similarly, if students use representations such as the number line to subtract, then subtracting across zeros is not so difficult. An appropriate sequence of exercises must thus be based on the strategies and materials used by students.

Adding More than Two Numbers

Students who are working to achieve fluency in adding more than two numbers often come up against a barrier when they simply begin adding a string of numbers, starting with the first number in the string and proceeding straight through the numbers. As their sum grows larger so does the likelihood that they will become confused and make errors in mental math. By contrast, thoughtful use of the associative property for addition allows students to develop a variety of strategies for adding more than two numbers fluently. Reflect 4.11 invites you to solve an addition problem with five addends. Consider how many ways you could solve the problem, and then inspect the three solutions in figure 4.10.

Reflect 4.11

Solve 35 + 42 + 65 + 57 + 38 = ☐ in as many different ways as you can. If possible, give the problem to colleagues, and compare your solution strategies with theirs.

How are the strategies alike? How are they different?

How are your strategies similar to or different from the strategies shown in figure 4.10?

Each solution strategy in figure 4.10 uses place value to break numbers into tens and ones, but the order in which the numbers are added varies. Solutions A and B break each addend into tens and ones, while solution C considers each pair of two-digit numbers, adding the pairs in turn. Some adults, as well as more sophisticated students, are likely to reorder the numbers, looking for pairs of "compatible" two-digit numbers to add. For example, they might begin by adding 35 + 65, to give them 100, and 42 + 38, to give them 80, thus simplifying the problem to 100 + 80 + 57. Then they might even break 57 apart to make it is easier to add on, giving them 180 + 20 + 37 = 237.

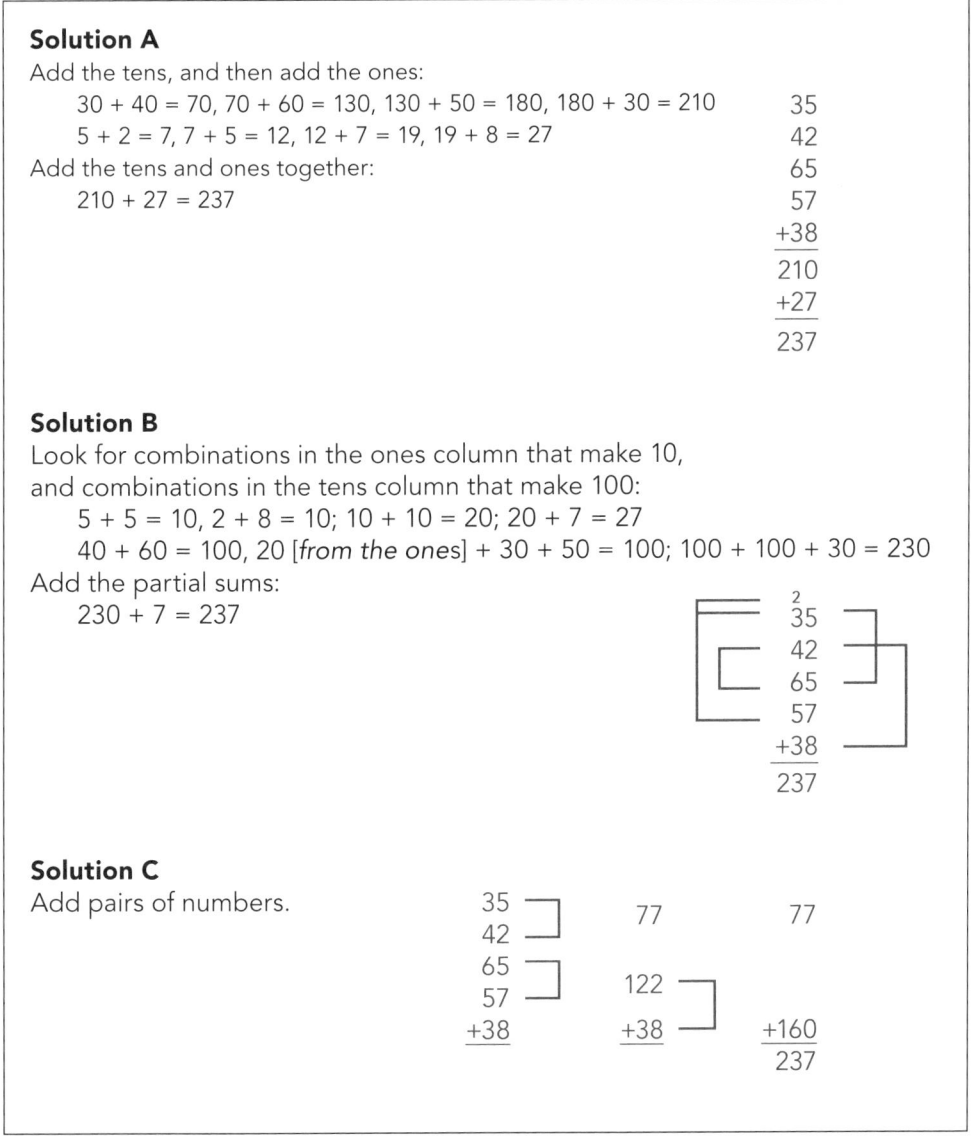

Solution A
Add the tens, and then add the ones:
  30 + 40 = 70, 70 + 60 = 130, 130 + 50 = 180, 180 + 30 = 210
  5 + 2 = 7, 7 + 5 = 12, 12 + 7 = 19, 19 + 8 = 27
Add the tens and ones together:
  210 + 27 = 237

```
     35
     42
     65
     57
    +38
    210
    +27
    237
```

Solution B
Look for combinations in the ones column that make 10,
and combinations in the tens column that make 100:
  5 + 5 = 10, 2 + 8 = 10; 10 + 10 = 20; 20 + 7 = 27
  40 + 60 = 100, 20 [*from the ones*] + 30 + 50 = 100; 100 + 100 + 30 = 230
Add the partial sums:
  230 + 7 = 237

```
         2
        35
        42
        65
        57
       +38
       237
```

Solution C
Add pairs of numbers.

```
  35            77          77
  42
  65
  57           122
 +38           +38        +160
                          237
```

Fig. 4.10. Three strategies for solving 35 + 42 + 65 + 57 + 38

Recognizing and Correcting Systematic Errors

Some students make mistakes consistently when adding or subtracting because they do not know the basic facts or they misremember a sum. Other students repeatedly stumble because their work is not well organized, perhaps because the columns are misaligned. Still other students do not understand the standard procedure for adding or subtracting and make systematic errors. How could you help students with these different kinds of problems? Pause to consider the questions in Reflect 4.12.

Reflect 4.12

How would you help a student who repeatedly gets the wrong answer in adding or subtracting because he or she—

- does not know the basic facts for addition and subtraction?
- is messy?
- makes systematic errors in using the standard procedure?

The appropriate instructional choice for helping particular students depends on the reason why they are making errors. The support that students need to learn their facts is very different from the support that they need to organize their work, for example. If you find that students do not know their facts, then you must carefully select appropriate thinking strategies, games, or other practice materials to help them learn the facts that they don't know. If you determine that students do not line up their numbers properly when adding, you might give them grid paper to assist in organizing their work. By itself, practice in adding or subtracting three-digit numbers is unlikely to result in more correct answers for students who are experiencing difficulties in remembering facts or working neatly.

Similarly, when your students are making systematic errors, you need to understand the source of the errors to determine how to help the students improve. Reflect 4.13 focuses on the work of three second-grade students who incorrectly added or subtracted three-digit numbers. Use the questions to guide your inspection of their work in figure 4.11.

Reflect 4.13

Consider the work of Barbara, Carlos, and Emma, shown in figure 4.11. Each of these second graders made an error systematically in adding or subtracting three-digit numbers.

Can you identify the error in each sample of work and apply it to a new problem?

How would you help each student overcome his or her error?

Barbara

245	856	619
+457	+178	+738
691	911	141

Carlos

123	238
586	482
+487	+399
1421	1821

Emma

$$6 \; \overset{7}{\cancel{8}} \, {}^{1}2 \qquad \overset{2}{\cancel{4}} \, {}^{1}3 \, {}^{1}3 \qquad \overset{7}{\cancel{8}} \, {}^{1}2 \, 9$$

$$-2\;5\;5 \qquad -2\;5\;6 \qquad -7\;7\;6$$

$$\;\;4\;2\;7 \qquad \;\;\;8\;7 \qquad \;\;\;5\;3$$

Fig. 4.11. Systematic errors in addition and subtraction in the work of three second-grade students

Each student consistently made a different error. Barbara and Carlos, the two students who were adding, recorded the tens digit when a column sum was greater than ten. Barbara did not regroup at all but simply ignored the ones digit in any two-digit column sum that she got. Carlos, by contrast, regrouped the ones digit in every two-digit sum that he obtained, treating it as a ten, and thereby arriving at some very improbable results. Emma, the student who was subtracting, regrouped correctly and got the correct answer when she had only one regrouping to make, but she came up with the wrong answer when she needed to regroup more than once.

These types of errors are common when students are taught an algorithm as a sequence of steps to memorize, without help in making strong links to conceptual understanding. Ways to address these sorts of systematic errors include discussion of whether answers are reasonable as well as revisiting the roles that place value and properties of addition play in adding and subtracting multi-digit numbers.

Using Incorrect Work to Build and Assess Understanding

Many students in the primary grades have difficulty in articulating their own reasoning and critiquing the arguments of their peers. In introducing students to the essential mathematical practice of critiquing the reasoning of others, starting with the work of a fictitious student is often wise—and none is better than a fictional character that happens to be your students' peer, presented in a classroom setting in an appealing work of children's literature. In this case, an ideal "fictitious student" is the fictional character Harley Harrison in *The Great Math Tattle Battle* (Bowen 2006). Harley Harrison is the best math student in his second-grade class—and the quickest to tattle on other students. But when a new student, Emma Jean, joins the class, Harley meets his match—in both math and tattling—and the "tattle battle" ensues.

Beth Kobett, one of the authors of the book in your hands, used Bowen's book to support students' developing understanding of two-digit addition and subtraction. *The Great Tattle Battle* provided an opportunity to have students critique and discuss the work of another student while building and demonstrating their own understanding, as shown in the vignette that follows.

> Ms. Kobett gathered students together and read *The Great Math Tattle Battle* (Bowen 2006) aloud to them. After she finished reading, she asked the students, "What mathematics did you notice in this story?"
>
> Lolowa remarked that Harley, in his tattles, "keeps track of everyone's mistakes—like the kid who was chewing erasers off pencils. Harley listed how many he chewed each day and added them."
>
> Sophia said, "He listed all the junk under two girls' desks and added up the stuff. That made the girls mad."
>
> Ms. Kobett then asked, "What happened when a new girl came into the class?"
>
> Lorin said, "She said that Harley had lots of math mistakes on his paper, and that made Harley upset. Then they both started to correct each other's papers."
>
> "So, let's take a look at one of Harley's papers," Ms. Kobett suggested, "and see if you can find any errors. Look carefully, as though you are Emma Jean or the teacher, and see if you can tell what Harley didn't do correctly."
>
> Ms. Kobett then distributed a sheet of problems supposedly solved by Harley Harrison (see fig. 4.12).

Figures 4.13–4.16 show some students' responses to the thinking that they detected in the answers to the problems in the set. Many students approached the task in the manner of the student whose work appears in figure 4.13, writing directly on the sheet and detailing what Harley had done in each case—the mistakes that he had made and how he should have solved the problems. Other students, like those whose work appears in figures 4.14–4.16, took a different approach. They wrote notes to Harley Harrison or Ms. Kobett about the solutions on the sheet and the apparent thinking behind them.

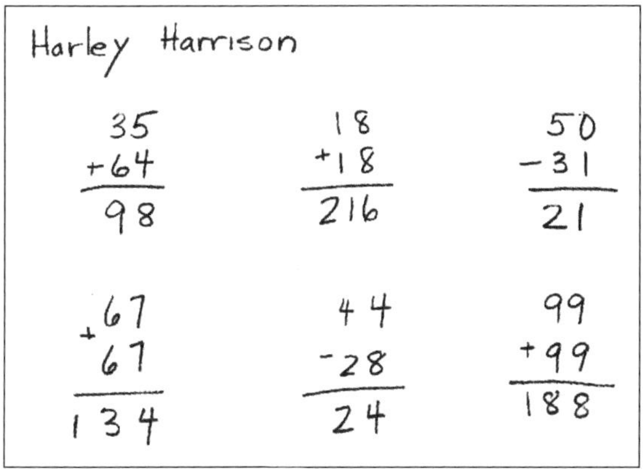

Fig. 4.12. A sheet showing addition and subtraction problems supposedly solved by
Harley Harrison in *The Great Math Tattle Battle* (Bowen 2006)

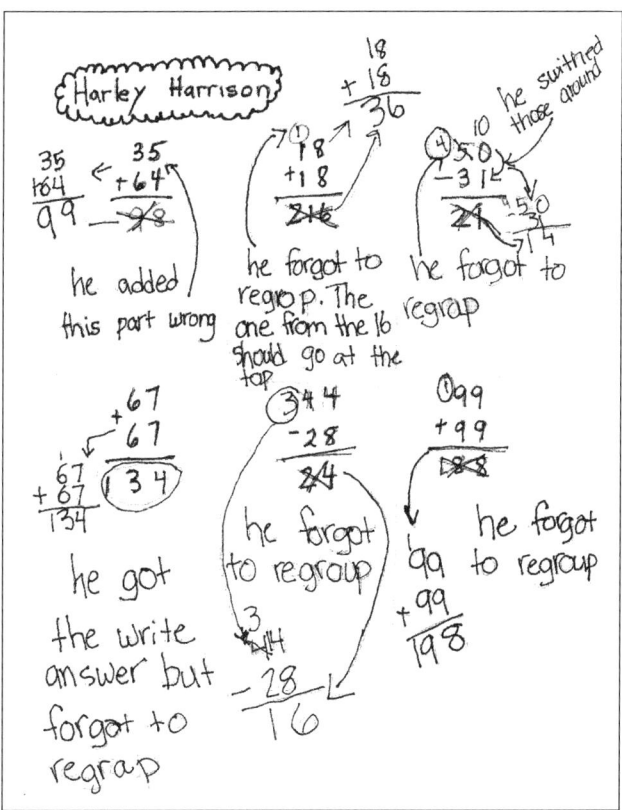

Fig. 4.13. A student's problem-by-problem critique of the work in figure 4.12,
detailing mistakes in the solutions

Dear Mrs. Kobett Harley
Harrison forgot to regroup on
#1 forgot to regroup on #2
also should have put the 1 from
the 16 at the top, on #3 he
forgot to regroup #4 he
got the right answer but
forgot to regroup on #5 he
forgot to regroup and #6
he forgot to regroup!
REGROUP HARLEY HARRISON!
Signed Emma Jean

Fig. 4.14. A note detailing errors and offering advice, by a student writing as Emma Jean

Dear, Mrs Kobett
   Harley Harrison got alot
wrong becvase he was focosing on tatalling
that is why he got alot wrong. And in the
story it said he was the bestin 2d grade
for math. So I bet if stopped focusing on
tatalling he could get all of them right.

Fig. 4.15. A note from a student suggesting that adding two-digit numbers requires
more than "focusing on totaling"

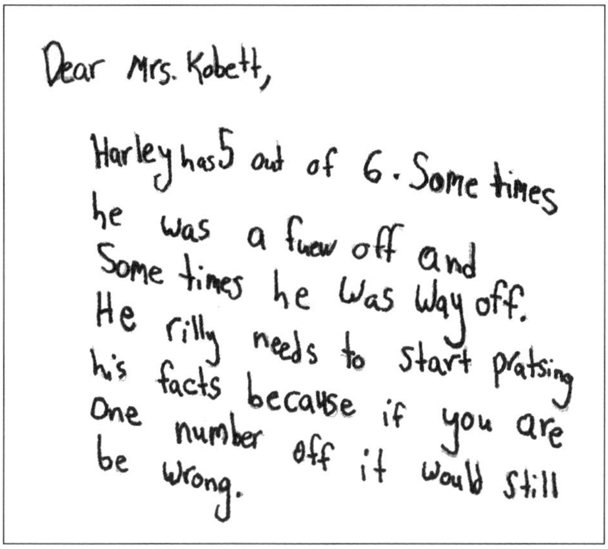
Dear Mrs. Kobett,

Harley has 5 out of 6. Some times
he was a fuew off and
Some times he Was Way off.
He rilly needs to start pratsing
h.'s facts because if you are
One number off it would still
be wrong.

Fig. 4.16. A note from a student philosophizing on the importance of knowing the basic facts

Fig. 4.14 shows a critique in the form of a note to Ms. Kobett from a student who imaginatively entered the fictional world of *The Great Tattle Battle* (Bowen 2006). Assuming the persona of Emma Jean, this student carefully and energetically ticked off Harley's failures to regroup, wrapping up her analysis with some sharply worded advice: "REGROUP HARLEY HARRISON!"

Figure 4.15 shows another critique in note form, this time from a student who suggested that Harley performed poorly on the problems because he was "focusing on totaling." By this, the student may have meant that Harley typically failed to regroup but just added or subtracted the numbers that appeared in a column. Questioning this student more closely might have elicited more information about his exact meaning and perhaps revealed whether he realized that Harley did have one correct answer.

The student whose work appears in figure 4.16 gave Harley a numerical score for his work: "Harley has 5 out of 6." In this case, the score gives the number of wrong, rather than right, answers out of the total number, meaning that Harley had 5 out 6 answers wrong—an accurate assessment of the work. This student zeroed in on Harley's need to master his basic facts, emphasizing that a "near miss" with a fact—being off even by just 1, as in the first problem, where Harley added 5 + 4 in the ones column and got 8—gives an answer that will "still be wrong."

Reflecting on Harley's work and deciphering it led to a real breakthrough about the need to regroup for many students in the class. They had to decide whether

Harley had made a mistake, and if so, what he had done and why. By exploring a fictitious student's methods (in this case, the methods of a fictional character who was vividly alive in their imaginations), and evaluating the techniques as correct or incorrect, they became aware of some useful strategies to try as well as some unsuccessful ones to avoid. The process of grading another's paper helped the children think ahead about the process and what to do. Reflect 4.14 offers an opportunity to think further about the value of the instructional approach illustrated in the classroom vignette.

Reflect 4.14

Beth Kobett gave students a sample of two-digit adding and subtracting problems from a fictitious student—in this case, a character in a children's book—to critique and evaluate.

How is this teaching approach different from sharing one particular procedure with students?

Summary: Learners, Curriculum, Instruction, and Assessment

To be effective in teaching students to add and subtract multi-digit numbers, you must have appropriate knowledge of learners, curriculum, instruction, and assessment. You need to know where your students are in their understanding of place value, fact strategies, use of computational strategies (such as compensation or decomposition), and fluency. Computational fluency develops along with increasing understanding of place value, and introducing the standard algorithms too early results in not enough sense making. Allowing your students to invent strategies first and engaging them in mental math (computational estimation) before they use paper-and-pencil algorithms are important. The situations and numbers in particular problems and the models used for solving them may affect the problems' difficulty for students and predispose them to use particular solution strategies. Students should begin by using models—straws, craft sticks, or connecting cubes, for example—that require them to make (*compose*) and break apart (*decompose*) their own groups of 10 and 100. When students' understanding of place value has developed sufficiently, they can begin to use manipulatives that have already been pre-grouped for them, such as base-ten blocks. Manipulative materials and representations that do not show the unit, such as chips or an open number line, are still more difficult for students because they are nonproportional.

As a teacher in the primary grades, you need not only to be familiar with common invented strategies but also to be able to understand student descriptions of new strategies and to determine whether a new strategy always works. You must be able to create story problems involving all problem types, with unknowns in all positions. Emphasizing place value and the properties of addition as students move toward the use of the standard algorithm is essential. Finally, by paying attention to students' use of various strategies, you can gain valuable information that helps you know how to build fluency and deeper understanding of the big ideas.

Conclusion

This chapter has focused on approaches to building and reinforcing students' understanding of two- and three-digit addition and subtraction. The concepts and skills that students need to have for this work grow out of and extend those that they develop gradually and naturally as they move through the years from prekindergarten to grade 2. First, they need to count and think about sets and part-whole relations; Chapter 1 discussed productive practices for promoting this learning. Working with problems set in story contexts usefully extends their understanding, as detailed in Chapter 2. To solve problems efficiently and confidently, they need to master basic addition and subtraction facts; Chapter 3 emphasized the value of first inventing their own strategies and then understanding and using common basic fact strategies. Chapter 4 has looked at fruitful ways to extend and apply this work in teaching two- and three-digit addition and subtraction meaningfully, in ways that encourage students to reason about and make sense of what they are doing.

Chapter 5—the final chapter in this book—frames the previous chapters' discussions of helping students develop the essential understandings that are appropriate for prekindergarten–grade 2 by looking back and ahead—mostly ahead, at the later development of these ideas in the mathematics that students will encounter as they move through school.

Chapter 5
Looking Back and Looking Ahead with Addition and Subtraction

This chapter highlights how the big ideas and essential understandings discussed in Chapters 1–4 align with ideas that students develop before their years in pre-kindergarten–grade 2 and in the years that follow as they progress in school. The chapter begins with a discussion of foundational understandings that students are expected to have on entering prekindergarten or kindergarten. When you encounter students in your prekindergarten–grade 2 classes who have gaps in their knowledge, you need to assess their understanding of the ideas that this first section highlights. The second section rounds out the chapter with a discussion of the connections of the ideas and understandings that students develop in prekindergarten–grade 2—the concepts and skills discussed in Chapters 1–4—with mathematics that students learn beyond second grade. This discussion demonstrates how important it is for student in prekindergarten–grade 2 to develop a deep understanding of the essential concepts that serve as a foundation for subsequent learning.

Foundational Knowledge for Addition and Subtraction in Pre-K–Grade 2

As young children learn to count, they also build experiences with putting sets of objects together and taking them apart. They learn about adding on and taking away, and they use counting to help them solve these types of problems with numbers less than or equal to 8. Some aspects of number that are particularly important for parents and teachers to emphasize include counting, subitizing (recognizing small quantities without counting), decomposing numbers into parts, and using written number symbols. The use of the number line to locate the positions of numbers on the line will aid students in their later use of the number line to add and subtract numbers. This work also links with their early understanding of a unit—particularly a unit of measurement—as they recognize that the number line is a length marked off into particular units. Children also begin to realize that, as the unit changes, so does the count or measure. Even at this early stage, the number line should show the zero to give young children a point of reference for the other units, so that "5" labels a length that is five equal units from zero.

Extending Knowledge of Addition and Subtraction in Grades 3–12

Addition and subtraction form the foundation for much of the mathematics learning that takes place in higher grades. Students continue to use these operations with various types of numbers and in varying contexts. They also extend these understandings and skills to the study of algebra in middle school and high school.

The work that students do with base-ten materials in prekindergarten–grade 2 lays a foundation for understanding place value and the properties of addition and subtraction—understanding that continues to be important as they extend their work with these operations to larger numbers, fractions, and decimals in grades 3–5. Figure 5.1 shows relevant standards for grades 3 and 4 in the Number and Operations in Base Ten (NBT) domain in the Common Core State Standards for Mathematics (CCSSM; National Governors Association Center for Best Practices and Council of Chief State School Officers [NGA Center and CCSSO] 2010). Students continue their use of invented or standard algorithms for addition and subtraction of whole numbers as they progress to decimals (to hundredths in grade 5) and rational numbers (including integers and signed decimals in grade 7).

Many students in grades 3–5 have difficulty with simple mental computations, such as 357 + 200 = □. When asked to use base-ten blocks to solve the problem, they have no difficulty in finding the answer, but they lack facility in using place value concepts, and as a result they are unable to find the answer mentally. Many times this is the consequence of an instructional emphasis on the standard algorithm too early in the students' development of understanding. The premature introduction of the algorithm, before students are able to make sense of it, sometimes results in their thinking of the numbers in a problem as individual digits instead of recognizing their actual values by applying place value concepts. In this situation, students often resort to using the standard algorithms even when numbers are easy to add or subtract mentally.

Common Core State Standards for Mathematics

Grade 3 (3.NBT.2)

2. Fluently add and subtract within 1000 using strategies and algorithms based on place value, properties of operations, and/or the relationship between addition and subtraction.

Grade 4 (4.NBT.4)

4. Fluently add and subtract multi-digit whole numbers using the standard algorithm.

Fig. 5.1. CCSSM standards for fluency in addition and subtraction for grades 3 and 4 (NGA Center and CCSSO 2010, pp. 24, 29)

The use of the number line to model addition and subtraction of whole numbers establishes an important foundation for representing larger numbers, decimals, fractions and mixed numbers, integers, and rational numbers on the number line. The number line is also an important tool in algebra, where it is used to graph solutions to inequalities. Representing addition and subtraction as jumps on the number line in prekindergarten–grade 2 builds toward representing addition and subtraction of integers on a number line later, as illustrated in figure 5.2.

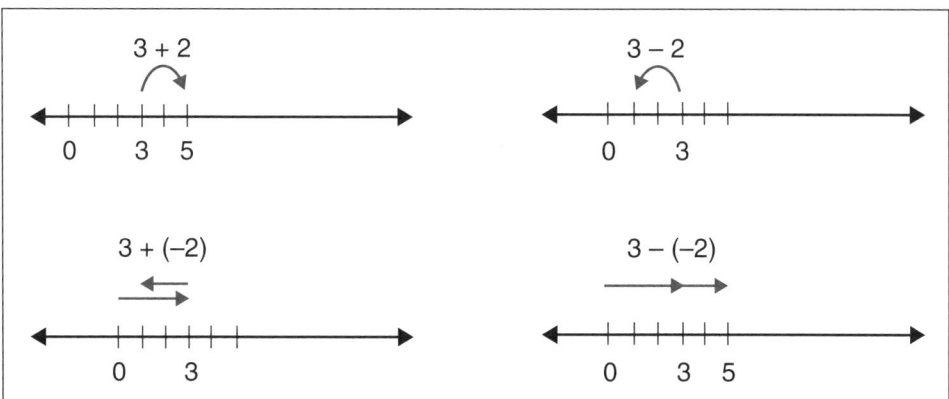

Fig. 5.2. Adding and subtracting on a number line, progressing to work with integers

Students in grade 6 use the number line as they learn about absolute value, the distance from zero of a signed number. This work also leads to applications involving coordinate graphing in grades 5–12 and reading scales on rulers and other measurement tools. In the middle grades, students may also be asked to use variables to determine where points are on a number line, in tasks like those shown in figure 5.3.

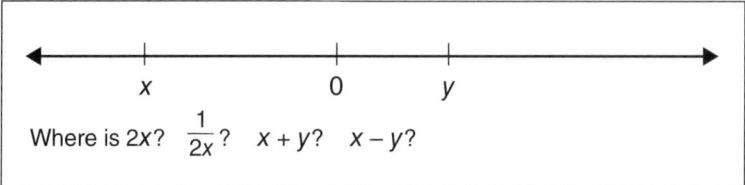

Fig. 5.3. Number line problems for students in the middle grades

Much of what students learn about addition and subtraction in the primary grades helps them in learning about multiplication and division in grades 3–6. Learning about properties of the operations of addition and subtraction in the early years leads to examination of the properties of multiplication and division in grade 3 and beyond. Using place value and the properties to make sense of adding and subtracting multi-digit numbers is useful preparation for multiplying and dividing. Knowing doubles addition facts makes learning the multiplication facts for 2 much easier. Being comfortable with addition and subtraction is helpful in solving problems about equal groups. Students must be able to add and subtract to multiply and divide multi-digit whole numbers.

In grade 4, students learn to add and subtract fractions with like denominators. They continue to use the notions first learned in the primary grades that one can combine only like objects: ones and ones, tens and tens, hundreds and hundreds, or fifths and fifths, eighths and eighths. In grade 5, they add and subtract fractions and mixed numbers that refer to the same whole or unit but have unlike denominators, learning that they must first restate them as equivalent fractions with identical denominators, to have like quantities to add or subtract. Students will extend and apply this idea later as they combine like terms in algebra.

Measurement provides many opportunities not only for solving problems involving addition and subtraction but also for making important connections with numerous ideas in mathematics. Using a ruler is akin to using a number line, and iterating units is similar to making a one-to-one correspondence. In grade 3, students will apply addition concepts as they learn about perimeter. They will also learn that area, volume, and angle measurements are additive—that is, that they can divide an object into parts, use the same unit to measure each part, and then add the measurements together to find the total. Figure 5.4 illustrates this idea.

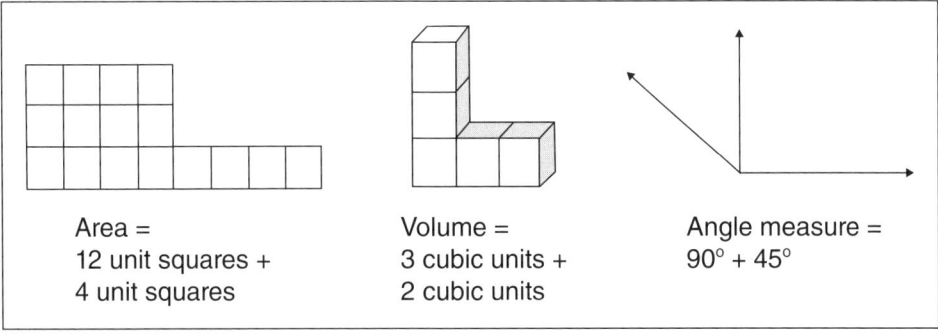

Area =
12 unit squares +
4 unit squares

Volume =
3 cubic units +
2 cubic units

Angle measure =
90° + 45°

Fig. 5.4. The additivity of area, volume, and angle measurements

In grades 3–5, students apply their understanding of addition and subtraction in solving problems and identifying and explaining patterns. They also apply addition and subtraction concepts in conjunction with other operations to solve data problems and represent data as detailed in CCSSM; figure 5.5 shows a grade 3 standard in the domain Measurement and Data.

Common Core State Standards for Mathematics

Grade 3 (3.MD.3)

3. Draw a scaled picture graph and a scaled bar graph to represent a data set with several categories. Solve one- and two-step "how many more" and "how many less" problems, using information presented in scaled bar graphs.

Fig. 5.5. CCSSM standard for representing and interpreting data for grade 3 (NGA Center and CCSSO 2010, p. 25)

Probably the most significant and important extension of addition and subtraction that students make comes when they begin to study algebra. As students create and solve equations with unknowns, they must recognize the same types of contexts for these operations in the new setting. Consider the following task, which is appropriate for students in grade 1 or 2:

Task: Jack's Birthday Candles

Jack is 7 years old. How many candles has he had on his birthday cakes since he was born?

Figure 5.6 shows work on this task by a student in the primary grades.

How can we find out?

$1+2+3+4+5+6+7+8+=29$

28 candles

Fig. 5.6. Work by a student in the primary grades on Jack's Birthday Candles

Students in first or second grade might use a picture, as in the figure. (It is interesting to note that the student whose work is shown drew pictures of cakes and candles for all of Jack's birthdays and recorded the correct total number of candles [28] beside the human figure drawn to the left of the first cake, but then she wrote a number sentence that included an extra addend [8] and gave an incorrect sum [29].)

Other students in the same grades might use the "sum to 10" strategy and solve the problem in the following way:

$$7 + 6 + 5 + 4 + 3 + 2 + 1 = 10 + 10 + 5 + 2 + 1 = 28$$

But what happens as Jack grows older? What is the total number of candles that Jack has had on his cakes when he has his eighth, ninth, tenth, and eleventh birthdays? Students in grades 3–5 might explore this question in a table, as shown in figure 5.7.

Jack's age	7	8	9	10	11
Total number of candles on Jack's birthday cakes	28	36	45	55	66

Fig. 5.7. The total number of candles on Jack's birthday cakes as his age changes from 7 to 8, 9, 10, and 11

As long as students consider the relationship between Jack's age and the total number of candles on his birthday cakes year by year, figuring out the total number of candles to date remains a fairly simple matter—at least for a few years. But how many candles has Jack had on all his birthday cakes by the time he is 21? Or 35? Or 60? At this point more advanced students can turn to algebra for help.

By looking for a pattern in the data in the table, students might notice that—

$$\text{at age 7, Jack has had 28 candles:} \quad 28 = \frac{7 \times 8}{2} ;$$

$$\text{at age 8, Jack has had 36 candles:} \quad 36 = \frac{8 \times 9}{2} ;$$

$$\text{at age 9, Jack has had 45 candles:} \quad 45 = \frac{9 \times 10}{2} ;$$

$$\text{at age 10, Jack has had 55 candles:} \quad 55 = \frac{10 \times 11}{2} ;$$

$$\text{at age 11, Jack has had 66 candles:} \quad 66 = \frac{11 \times 12}{2} .$$

So—

$$\text{at age 21, Jack has had } \frac{21 \times 22}{2} = 231 \text{ candles on his cakes;}$$

$$\text{at age 35, Jack has had } \frac{35 \times 36}{2} = 630 \text{ candles on his cakes; and}$$

$$\text{at age 60, Jack has had } \frac{60 \times 61}{2} = 1830 \text{ candles on his cakes.}$$

Furthermore, in general,

$$\text{at age } A \text{, Jack has had } \frac{A \times (A+1)}{2} = \frac{A^2 + A}{2} \text{ candles on his cakes.}$$

Students in the primary grades frequently encounter another type of problem that readies them for subsequent work in algebra. Problems in which they must decompose a whole into two parts and consider possible numbers for the parts set the stage for later work with one or two variables. Consider the following task.

Task: How Many Apples? How Many Pears?

A plate has just two kinds of fruit on it—apples and pears—and it has 7 pieces of fruit in all. How many pieces of fruit might be apples, and how many might be pears?

To solve the problem, students must make all the combinations of numbers of apples and pears that give them 7 pieces of fruit in all:

1 apple and 6 pears

2 apples and 5 pears

3 apples and 4 pears

4 apples and 3 pears

5 apples and 2 pears

6 apples and 1 pear

They need to recognize that "6 apples and 1 pear" is the same as "1 pear and 6 apples" and that the list above exhausts the possible combinations of apples and pears on the plate.

Children's literature is often a good resource for such problems. *The Napping House* (Wood 2009), for example, begins with Granny sleeping, and, one after another, various people and animals join her. A task like the following can be set in this story context.

Task: Napping Creatures

If 12 creatures are napping in the house, how many of them might be people, and how many might be animals?

(Based on *The Napping House* [Wood 2009])

Such stories often provide opportunities for students to make tables and look for mathematical patterns. For instance, at one point, there are 24 feet in the house in

The Napping House. Who might be in the house? Figure 5.8 shows samples of students' work in response to this question.

Fig. 5.8. Two samples of student work on Napping Creatures

The changing number of creatures in the house sets up an opportunity for natural use of a variable. Students can create a table showing the number of creatures and the number of feet in the house as the story progresses.

Conclusion

Addition and subtraction are pervasive in everyday and school experience from the time that children are very young all the way through high school and beyond. Children begin solving addition and subtraction problems simply by counting, using small numbers and actual objects, and gradually increasing their ability to put groups together, take them apart, add to, take away, and compare. They apply the basic notions of addition and subtraction to decimals, fractions, and variables. They solve problems by using addition and subtraction, sometimes in conjunction with other operations. They use addition and subtraction as they perform multiplication and division computations. Building a deep understanding of the big ideas and essential understandings of addition and subtraction in prekindergarten–grade 2 is indispensable for students' future mathematical success.

Appendix 1
The Big Ideas and Essential Understandings for Addition and Subtraction

This book focuses on the big ideas and essential understandings that are identified and discussed in *Developing Essential Understanding of Addition and Subtraction for Teaching Mathematics in Prekindergarten–Grade 2* (Caldwell, Karp, and Bay-Williams 2011). For the reader's convenience, the complete list of the big ideas and essential understandings in that book is reproduced below.

Big Idea 1. Addition and subtraction are used to represent and solve many different kinds of problems.

Essential Understanding 1*a*. Addition and subtraction of whole numbers are based on sequential counting with whole numbers.

Essential Understanding 1*b*. Subtraction has an inverse relationship with addition.

Essential Understanding 1*c*. Many different problem situations can be represented by part-part-whole relationships and addition or subtraction.

Essential Understanding 1*d*. Part-part-whole relationships can be expressed by using number sentences like $a + b = c$ or $c - b = a$, where a and b are the parts and c is the whole.

Essential Understanding 1*e*. The context of a problem situation and its interpretation can lead to different representations.

Big Idea 2. The mathematical foundations for understanding computational procedures for addition and subtraction of whole numbers are the properties of addition and place value.

Essential Understanding 2*a*. The commutative and associative properties for addition of whole numbers allow computations to be performed flexibly.

Essential Understanding 2*b*. Subtraction is not commutative or associative for whole numbers.

Essential Understanding 2c. Place-value concepts provide a convenient way to compose and decompose numbers to facilitate addition and subtraction computations.

Essential Understanding 2d. Properties of addition are central in justifying the correctness of computational algorithms.

Appendix 2
Resources for Teachers

The following list highlights a few of the many books, articles, videos, and websites that are helpful resources for teaching addition and subtraction in prekindergarten–grade 2. Abstracts from the publishers provide brief descriptions of some of the resources.

Books

Battista, Michael T. *Cognition-Based Assessment & Teaching of Addition and Subtraction: Building on Students' Reasoning.* Portsmouth, N.H.: Heinemann, 2012.

Using a research-based framework that describes the development of students' thinking and learning in terms of levels of sophistication, a "cognitive terrain" that includes ascents and plateaus, Battista shows how teachers can build on their students' reasoning.

Caldwell, Janet H., Karen Karp, and Jennifer M. Bay-Williams. *Developing Essential Understanding of Addition and Subtraction for Teaching Mathematics in Prekindergarten–Grade 2.* Essential Understanding Series. Reston, Va.: National Council of Teachers of Mathematics, 2011.

"Unpacking" the ideas related to addition and subtraction is a critical step in developing a deeper understanding. To those without specialized training, many of these ideas might appear to be easy to teach. But those who teach in prekindergarten–grade 2 are aware of their subtleties and complexities. This book identifies and examines two big ideas and related essential understandings for teaching early addition and subtraction. The authors examine the ways in which counting leads to addition and subtraction, as well as the role that these operations play in more advanced topics. The discussion highlights challenges in teaching, learning, and assessment and is interspersed with questions for teachers' reflection.

Carpenter, Thomas, Elizabeth Fennema, Megan Loef Franke, Linda Levi, and Susan B. Empson. *Children's Mathematics/Cognitively Guided Instruction.* Portsmouth, N.H.: Heinemann, 1999.

By the time children begin school, most have already developed a sophisticated, informal understanding of basic mathematical concepts and problem-solving strategies. Too often, however, the mathematics that classroom instruction imposes on them fails to connect with this informal knowledge. The authors developed this book to help teachers understand children's intuitive mathematical thinking and use that knowledge to guide students in learning mathematics with understanding. Based on more than twenty years of research, the book portrays the development of children's understanding of basic number concepts. The authors offer a detailed explanation and numerous examples of the problem-solving and computational processes that virtually all children use as their numerical thinking develops. They also describe how classrooms can be organized to foster that development. Two accompanying CDs include videos that provide an inside look at students and teachers in real classrooms implementing the teaching and learning strategies described in the text.

Fosnot, Catherine, and Maarten Dolk. *Young Mathematicians at Work: Constructing Number Sense, Addition, and Subtraction.* Portsmouth, N.H.: Heinemann, 2001.

Fosnot and Dolk focus on the way in which children between the ages of four and eight construct their knowledge of the operations of addition and subtraction. The authors—

- emphasize that a deep knowledge of number sense will support students' computational skills;

- provide strategies to help teachers turn their classrooms into math workshops that encourage and reflect mathematizing;

- explore the development of a repertoire of strategies;

- define and give examples of the use of an open number line model; and

- discuss calculation using number sense and the role of algorithms in instruction about computation.

O'Connell, Susan, and John SanGiovanni. *Mastering the Basic Math Facts in Addition and Subtraction: Strategies, Activities, and Interventions to Move Students beyond Memorization.* Portsmouth, N.H.: Heinemann, 2011.

O'Connell and SanGiovanni emphasize the value of helping students develop both automaticity with the facts and understanding of them instead of merely memorizing them. Aligning their ideas with both the Common Core State Standards and the NCTM Principles and Standards, the authors stress the importance of understanding the concepts of addition and subtraction. They share insights into teaching the basic facts, including a variety of instructional strategies and activities.

Van de Walle, John A., Karen S. Karp, and Jennifer M. Bay-Williams. *Elementary and Middle School Mathematics: Teaching Developmentally.* 8th ed. Boston: Pearson, 2013.

The purpose of this book is to help teachers understand mathematics and become confident in their ability to teach the subject to children in kindergarten through eighth grade. The chapters related to teaching and learning basic facts and addition and subtraction provide ideas and insights that will support teachers as they design and implement their lessons.

Articles

Baroody, Arthur. "Why Children Have Difficulties Mastering the Basic Number Combinations and How to Help Them." *Teaching Children Mathematics* 13 (August 2006): 22–31.

In this well-known article, Baroody discusses the three phases through which children progress in gaining mastery of addition and subtraction number combinations: (1) using counting strategies, (2) using reasoning strategies, and (3) producing correct answers efficiently (mastery). He shares several vignettes that contrast "conventional wisdom" and "the number-sense view."

Bofferding, Laura, Melissa Kemmerle, and Aki Murata. "Making 10 My Way." *Teaching Children Mathematics* 19 (October 2012): 164–73.

The authors describe a kindergarten unit of study that focuses on identifying combinations of 10 by using ten frames and counters. Students receive explicit instruction on addition and subtraction problem types, including "join" (result unknown), "compare" (difference unknown), "separate" (result unknown), and "part-part-whole" (part unknown or whole unknown). Samples of students' work are shared to highlight the strategies that the kindergartners used, and a table that includes activity descriptions, needed materials, and goals shows how to differentiate instruction.

Buchholz, Lisa. "Learning Strategies for Addition and Subtraction Facts: The Road to Fluency and the License to Think." *Teaching Children Mathematics* 10 (March 2004): 362–69.

This article suggests strategies to offer students to help them establish and retain addition and subtraction facts, including the use of doubles, combinations that sum to 10, and "fact families," as well as "doubles plus 1" and "doubles minus 1" (or plus or minus 2), "count up," "add 1 to 9," "add 10," "count back," "think addition," and "subtract from 10." A worthwhile discussion deals with a parent's initial wish to have her son learn more about "borrowing" and "carrying."

Griffin, Sharon. "Laying the Foundation for Computational Fluency in Early Childhood." *Teaching Children Mathematics* 9 (February 2003): 306–9.

Drawing on research on number sense and the use of strategies, the author provides a diagnostic tool for determining where students are in their thinking about a basic addition situation. The tool distinguishes five levels of possible performance by students, ranging from those who do not know how to respond to a basic situation to those who use retrieval strategies efficiently. The author shares a series of instructional "next steps" to help students who are performing at a particular level advance to the next one.

Mann, Rebecca L. "Balancing Act: The Truth behind the Equals Sign." *Teaching Children Mathematics* 11 (September 2004): 65–69.

This article moves students from considering the equal sign as a signal that the answer is coming next to a symbol that indicates a "balanced," or equivalent, relationship between the quantities on the two sides of an equation. Building on a discussion of seesaws, students model the actions of seesaws that have them sitting on one end as different imaginary items are placed in their hands. Teacher and students create a set of generalizations that help students see the connection with the equal sign. The author includes challenging activities that might be successful with students who finish early or are gifted.

Postlewait, Kristian B., Michelle R. Adams, and Jeffrey C. Shih. "Promoting Meaningful Mastery of Addition and Subtraction." *Teaching Children Mathematics* 9 (February 2003): 354–57.

The authors posit that students' ability to compose and decompose number is a basis for computational fluency, and they argue that this skill allows students to move away from a reliance on rules and procedures to a conceptual understanding of number and operations.

Wenrick, Melanie, Jean L. Behrand, and Laura C. Mohs. "A Pathway for Mathematical Practices." *Teaching Children Mathematics* 19 (February 2013): 354–62.

The authors show students exploring the commutative property of addition, the decomposition of numbers, relationships among numbers, and the meaning of the equal sign. First, the students decide whether equations are true or false, and then they rewrite equations that are false to make them true. Students share strategies as they discuss their thinking about how they solved the problems. The authors highlight the importance of selecting appropriate problems for use in instruction, and they share several examples of student work that offer opportunities for students to discuss the work of others.

Wicket, Maryann. "Tuheen's Thinking about Place Value." *Teaching Children Mathematics* 16 (November 2009): 256.

Students who were given the expression "59 + 67 =" (written horizontally in this way) were asked to solve the problem by using any strategy that made sense to them and that they could explain. Although the students were familiar with the standard algorithm, several found the regrouping process challenging. A sample of work by one student, Tuheen, together with a detailed account of his thinking and his written record, is perfect to share with a class as the basis for discussion.

Videos

Integrating Mathematics and Pedagogy (IMAP)

http://www.sci.sdsu.edu/CRMSE/IMAP/video.html

IMAP: Select Videos of Children's Reasoning is a CD containing twenty-five video clips of elementary school children engaged in mathematical thinking. The CD runs on both PC and Mac platforms and comes with an interface that includes the transcript (full or synchronized) and background information for each clip. Also included on the CD is a video guide containing questions to consider before and after viewing each video clip, interviews that teachers or prospective teachers can use when working with children, and other resources.

See also Carpenter and colleagues (1999), under "Books."

Children's Mathematics/Cognitively Guided Instruction has two accompanying CDs that provide an inside look at students and teachers in real classrooms implementing the teaching and learning strategies described in the text.

Online Resources

NCTM Illuminations Lessons

http://illuminations.nctm.org/Lessons.aspx

The NCTM Illuminations website has hundreds of lessons. Select the type of lessons that you want as well as the appropriate grade band, and click Search.

Illustrative Mathematics Project

http://www.illustrativemathematics.org

Illustrative Mathematics provides guidance to states, assessment consortia, testing companies, and curriculum developers by illustrating the range and types of mathematical work that support implementation of the Common Core State Standards. One tool on this website is a growing collection of mathematical tasks that are organized by standard for each grade level and illustrate each standard's important features. The tasks on the website are not meant to be considered in isolation but are presented in sets that illustrate a particular standard. Eventually, the site will showcase sets of tasks for each standard that—

- illuminate the central meaning of the standard and also show connections with other standards;

- clarify what is familiar about the standard and what is new with the advent of the Common Core;

- include both teaching and assessment tasks; and

- reflect the full range of difficulty expected.

Thinking Blocks: Addition and Subtraction

www.thinkingblocks.com/ThinkingBlocks_AS/TB_AS_ Main.html

Thinking Blocks are teacher-developed tools that link to the various problem structures. They use two-digit numbers and problems with multiple steps, including "compare," "part-part-whole," and "change" examples. Because the ideas are presented as games, viewing the introduction is a necessary preliminary for playing.

Appendix 3
Tasks

This book examines rich tasks that have been used in the classroom to bring to the surface students' understandings and misunderstandings about addition and subtraction. A sampling of these tasks is offered here, in the order in which they appear in the book. At More4U, Appendix 3 includes these tasks and others, some with templates for classroom use.

Count, Sort, Compare

Instructions for the teacher: Put objects in bags (no more than 10 items for very young students). Each collection of objects should have multiple "copies" of some objects. Give students time to organize and count the items. Then pose questions to help them reflect on their counting and sorting and make comparisons of numbers of objects:

- "How did you organize your items?"

- "Why did you organize your items that way?"

- "What item do you have the greatest number of in your bag?"

- "What item do you have the smallest number of in your bag?"

- "Who has the same number of [*particular items*] as [*a particular student*]?"

- "Who has more [*particular items*] than [*a particular student*]? How many more?"

- "Who has fewer [*particular items*] than [*a particular student*]? How many fewer?"

- "How many items do you and [*a particular student*] have together?"

- "Does anyone have two more [*particular items*] than [*a particular student*]?"

How Can You Show _____?

Instructions for the teacher: Give each student or small group of students a small collection of blocks, counters, or other objects (no more than 10 items for very young students), along with a number that is less than or equal to the total number of objects. For example, you might give your students collections of 10 objects along with the number 7. Ask them to use the objects to make two groups that can be combined to produce the given number.

How Many Ways Can They Land?

Instructions for the teacher: Find a clean, empty can, and put in it a small collection of two-color counters (no more than 10 for very young children). If two-color counters are unavailable, spray-paint dried beans on one side (or color one side with a marker).

Have students shake the counters and roll them out onto a table or the floor.

Ask (if you are working with beans), "If you toss _____ beans, how many different ways can they land?"

Macaroni Squeeze Game

Instructions for the teacher: Let students explore unknown addends by "squeezing" uncooked, small noodles into two different-sized groups in small, clear, sealed sandwich bags. To make each bag, affix a piece of colored tape or draw a line with a permanent marker down the middle of the bag, as shown on the left below, or draw a circle on it, as shown on the right.

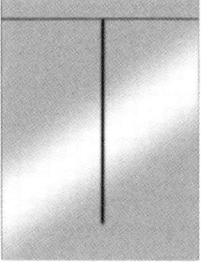

Put 7 noodles (or another number, up to 10) in each bag and seal it. Make as many bags as you need for your students.

Place the bags flat on a table or desk for the task. Have students move noodles to either side of the line (or in or out of the circle), as shown below, and record their results.

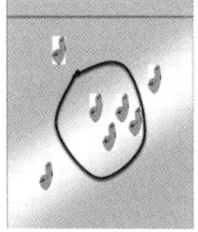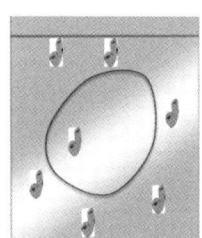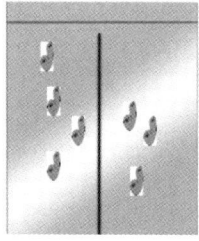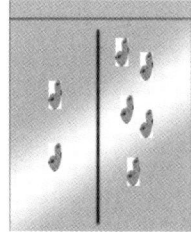

4 inside and 3 outside	1 inside and 6 outside	4 on the left and 3 on the right	2 on the left and 5 on the right
$4 + 3 = 7$	$1 + 6 = 7$	$4 + 3 = 7$	$2 + 5 = 7$

Hen and Egg Game

Instructions for the teacher: Use beans or other counters to represent eggs and a cup or a paper cutout of a chicken to represent a hen. Decide on a target number up to 10—say, 8—and arrange that number of beans, as eggs, on a table (see below).

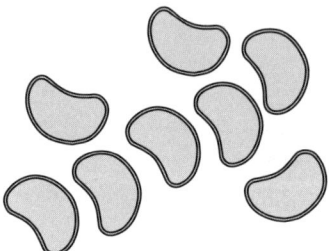

To begin, say, "There are 8 eggs in the whole nest," and count them aloud or ask a student to count them. Then move the "hen" to "sit on" some number of the "eggs," hiding them completely from view, as shown below.

Ask, "How many eggs is the hen sitting on?" Help your students to connect the language of part-part-whole to what they are seeing by saying, "You can count one of the parts, and you know what the whole is, but now you need to find the value of the missing part." Ask the students to name the part and the whole and find the missing part. Students can play this game in pairs, with one student using the cup or hen cutout to hide some of the eggs and asking the partner to name the missing part.

Dot Cards

Instructions for the teacher: Dot cards give students strong visual support for finding a missing addend. Make dot cards that give the whole and show one of the parts, as in the sample below.

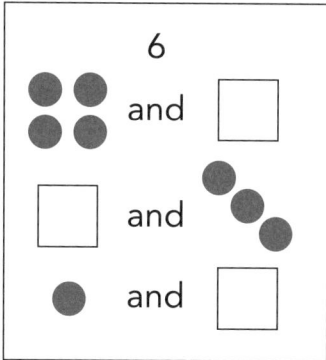

For a particular number on a dot card—say, 6, as in the sample above—ask,

Can you make 6 by adding two parts so that this sentence is true?

The part on the card + the missing part = 6

References

Citations for children's books discussed in the text appear in a separate section at the end of the reference list.

Baroody, Arthur. "Why Children Have Difficulties Mastering the Basic Number Combinations and How to Help Them." *Teaching Children Mathematics* 13 (August 2006): 22–31.

Baroody, Arthur, Neet Priva Bajwa, and Michael Eiland. "Why Can't Johnny Remember the Basic Facts?" *Developmental Disability Research Review* 15 (January 2009): 69–79.

Beckmann, Sybilla. "Solving Algebra and Other Story Problems with Simple Diagrams: A Method Demonstrated in Grade 4–6 Texts Used in Singapore." *Mathematics Educator* 14 (2004): 42–46.

Benoit, Laurent, Henri Lehalle, and François Jouen. "Do Young Children Acquire Number Words through Subitizing or Counting?" *Cognitive Development* 19 (July–September 2004): 291–307.

Caldwell, Janet H., Karen Karp, and Jennifer M. Bay-Williams. *Developing Essential Understanding of Addition and Subtraction for Teaching Mathematics in Prekindergarten–Grade 2*. Essential Understanding Series. Reston, Va.: National Council of Teachers of Mathematics, 2011.

Carpenter, Thomas P., Megan Loef Franke, and Linda Levi. *Thinking Mathematically: Integrating Arithmetic and Algebra in the Elementary School*. Portsmouth, N.H.: Heinemann, 2003.

Chapin, Suzanne H., and Art Johnson. *Math Matters: Understanding the Math You Teach, Grades K–8*. 2nd ed. Sausalito, Calif.: Math Solutions, 2006.

Clements, Douglas H. "Subitizing: What Is It? Why Teach It?" *Teaching Children Mathematics* 5 (March 1999): 400–405.

Clements, Douglas H., and Julie Sarama. *Learning and Teaching Early Math: The Learning Trajectories Approach*. 2nd ed. New York: Routledge, 2014.

Cognition and Technology Group at Vanderbilt. "Anchored Instruction and Its Relationship to Situated Cognition." *Educational Researcher* 19 (August/September 1990): 2–10.

Common Core State Standards Writing Team. Draft Progressions: K, Counting and Cardinality; K–5, Operations and Algebraic Thinking, 2011. http://commoncoretools .files.wordpress.com/2011/05/ccss_progression_cc_oa_k5_2011_05_302.pdf.

Crespo, Sandy, Andreas O. Kyriakides, and Shelly McGee. "Nothing 'Basic' about Basic Facts: Exploring Addition Facts with Fourth Graders." *Teaching Children Mathematics* 12 (September 2005): 60–67.

Dougherty, Barbara J. "Access to Algebra: A Process Approach." In *The Future of the Teaching and Learning of Algebra*, edited by Helen Chick, Kaye Stacey, Jill Vincent, and John Vincent, pp. 207–13. Melbourne, Victoria, Australia: University of Melbourne, 2001.

English, Lyn D. "Children's Problem Posing within Formal and Informal Contexts." *Journal for Research in Mathematics Education* 29 (January 1998): 83–106.

Fosnot, Catherine, and Maarten Dolk. *Young Mathematicians at Work: Constructing Number Sense, Addition, and Subtraction*. Portsmouth, N.H.: Heinemann, 2001.

Fuson, Karen, and Youngshim Kwon. "Korean Children's Single-Digit Addition and Subtraction: Numbers Structured by Ten." *Journal for Research in Mathematics Education* 23 (March 1992): 148–65.

Griffin, Cynthia C., and Asha K. Jitendra. "Word Problem-Solving Instruction in Inclusive Third-Grade Mathematics Classrooms." *Journal of Educational Research* 102 (January/February 2009): 187–201.

Grossman, Pamela. *The Making of a Teacher*. New York: Teachers College Press, 1990.

Hiebert, James, and Diana Wearne. "Instruction, Understanding, and Skill in Multidigit Addition and Subtraction." *Cognition and Instruction* 14, no. 3 (1996): 251–83.

Hill, Heather C., Brian Rowan, and Deborah Loewenberg Ball. "Effects of Teachers' Mathematical Knowledge for Teaching on Student Achievement." *American Educational Research Journal* 42 (Summer 2005): 371–406.

Hudson, Tom. "Correspondences and Numerical Differences between Disjoint Sets." *Child Development* 54 (February 1983): 84–90.

Kamii, Constance, and Barbara A. Lewis. "Single-Digit Subtraction with Fluency." *Teaching Children Mathematics* 10 (December 2003): 230–36.

Kamii, Constance, and Judith Rummelsburg. "Arithmetic for First Graders Lacking Number Concepts." *Teaching Children Mathematics* 14 (March 2008): 389–94.

Karp, Karen, Sarah Bush, and Barbara Dougherty. "Avoiding Rules That Expire." *Teaching Children Mathematics* 21 (August 2014): 18–25.

Kieran, Carolyn. "Algebraic Thinking in the Early Grades: What Is It?" *Mathematics Educator* 8 (April 2004): 139–51.

Magnusson, Shirley, Joseph Krajcik, and Hilda Borko. "Nature, Sources, and Development of Pedagogical Content Knowledge for Science Teaching." In *Examining Pedagogical Content Knowledge*, edited by Julie Gess-Newsome and Norman G. Lederman, pp. 95–132. Dordrecht, The Netherlands: Kluwer Academic, 1999.

Merseth, Katherine K. "How Old Is the Shepherd? An Essay about Mathematics Education." *Phi Delta Kappan* 74 (March 1993): 548–54.

National Governors Association Center for Best Practices and Council of Chief State School Officers (NGA Center and CCSSO). *Common Core State Standards for Mathematics. Common Core State Standards (College- and Career-Readiness Standards and K–12 Standards in English Language Arts and Math)*. Washington, D.C.: NGA Center and CCSSO, 2010. http://www.corestandards.org.

National Mathematics Advisory Panel. *Foundations for Success: The Final Report of the National Mathematics Advisory Panel*. Washington, D.C.: U.S. Department of Education, 2008.

National Research Council. *Reshaping School Mathematics: A Framework for Curriculum*. Washington, D.C.: National Academy Press, 1990.

———. *Adding It Up: Helping Children Learn Mathematics.* Mathematics Learning Study Committee, Jeremy Kilpatrick, Jane Swafford, and Bradford Findell, eds. Center for Education, Division of Behavioral and Social Sciences and Education. Washington, D.C.: National Academy Press, 2001.

O'Connell, Susan, and John SanGiovanni. *Mastering the Basic Math Facts in Addition and Subtraction: Strategies, Activities, and Interventions to Move Students beyond Memorization.* Portsmouth, N.H.: Heinemann, 2011.

Parmar, Rene S., John Cawley, and Richard Frazita. "Word Problem-Solving by Students with Mild Disabilities and Normally Achieving Students." *Exceptional Children* 61 (March/April 1996): 415–30.

Peltenburg, Marjolijn, Marja van den Heuvel-Panhuizen, and Alexander Robitzsch. "Special Education Students' Use of Indirect Addition in Solving Subtraction Problems Up to 100: A Proof of the Didactical Potential of an Ignored Procedure." *Educational Studies in Mathematics* 79, no. 3 (2012): 351–69.

Popham, W. James. "Defining and Enhancing Formative Assessment." Paper presented at the CCSSO State Collaborative on Assessment and Student Standards FAST meeting, Austin, Tex., October 10–13, 2006.

RAND Mathematics Study Panel. *Mathematical Proficiency for All Students: Toward a Strategic Research and Development Program in Mathematics Education.* Santa Monica, Calif.: RAND, 2003.

Sarama, Julie, and Douglas H. Clements. *Early Childhood Mathematics Education Research: Learning Trajectories for Young Children.* New York: Routledge, 2009.

Shih, Jeffrey, William R. Speer, and Beatrice C. Babbitt. "Instruction: Yesterday I Learned to Add; Today I Forgot." In *Achieving Fluency: Special Education and Mathematics,* edited by Francis (Skip) Fennell, pp. 59–83. Reston, Va.: National Council of Teachers of Mathematics, 2011.

Shulman, Lee S. "Those Who Understand: Knowledge Growth in Teaching." *Educational Researcher* 15, no. 2 (1986): 4–14.

———. "Knowledge and Teaching." *Harvard Educational Review* 57, no. 1 (1987): 1–22.

Van de Walle, John A., Karen S. Karp, and Jennifer M. Bay-Williams. *Elementary and Middle School Mathematics: Teaching Developmentally.* 8th ed. New York: Pearson, 2013.

Van de Walle, John A., Karen S. Karp, LouAnn H. Lovin, and Jennifer M. Bay-Williams. *Teaching Student-Centered Mathematics: Developmentally Appropriate Instruction for Grades 3–5.* Vol. 2. 2nd ed. New York: Pearson, 2014.

Verschaffel, Lieven, Brian Greer, and Erik de Corte. "Whole Number Concepts and Operations." In *Second Handbook of Research on Mathematics Teaching and Learning,* edited by Frank K. Lester, Jr., pp. 557–628. Charlotte, N.C.: Information Age; Reston, Va.: National Council of Teachers of Mathematics, 2007.

Wiliam, Dylan. "Keeping Learning on Track: Classroom Assessment and the Regulation of Learning." In *Second Handbook of Research on Mathematics Teaching and Learning,* edited by Frank K. Lester, Jr., pp. 1053–98. Charlotte, N.C.: Information Age; Reston, Va.: National Council of Teachers of Mathematics, 2007.

Xin, Yan Ping, Asha K. Jitendra, and Andria Deatline-Buchman. "Effects of Mathematical Word Problem-Solving Instruction on Middle School Students with Learning Problems." *Journal of Special Education* 39 (Fall 2005): 181–92.

Yinger, Robert J. "The Conversation of Teaching: Patterns of Explanation in Mathematics Lessons." Paper presented at the meeting of the International Study Association on Teacher Thinking, Nottingham, England, May 1998.

Children's Books

Anno, Mitsumasa. *Anno's Counting House*. New York: Philomel, 1982.

Bowen, Anne. *The Great Math Tattle Battle*. Morton Grove, Ill.: Albert Whitman, 2006.

Crews, Donald. *10 Black Dots*. New York: HarperCollins, 1995.

Cuyler, Margery. *Guinea Pigs Add Up*. New York: Walker, 2010.

Freeman, Don. *A Pocket for Corduroy*. New York: Penguin, 1978.

Hamm, Diane Johnson. *How Many Feet in the Bed?* New York: Simon and Schuster, 1994.

Herman, Charlotte. *The Memory Cupboard: A Thanksgiving Story*. Morton Grove, Ill.: Albert Whitman, 2003.

Kellogg, Steven. *Jack and the Beanstalk*. New York: HarperCollins, 1997.

Neitzle, Shirley. *The Bag I Am Taking to Grandma's*. New York: William Morris, 1986.

Pallotta, Jerry. *The Icky Bug Counting Book*. Watertown, Mass.: Charlesbridge, 1991.

Parker, Kim. *Counting in the Garden*. New York: Orchard Books, 2005.

Pittman, Helena Clare. *Counting Jennie*. Minneapolis: Carolrhoda Books, 1994.

Schwartz, Alvin. *There Is a Carrot in My Ear and Other Noodle Tales*. New York: HarperCollins, 1982.

Seuss, Dr. (Theodor Seuss Geisel). *Ten Apples on Top!* New York: Random House, 1961.

Shaw, Nancy. *Sheep in a Jeep*. New York: Houghton Mifflin Harcourt, 1986.

Slobodkina, Esphyr. *Caps for Sale*. New York: HarperCollins, 1940.

Wood, Audrey. *The Napping House*. New York: Harcourt, 2009.